PRAISE FOR
MITCH CANTOR

"Mitch Cantor's concept of personal relationships with your customers, along with the willingness to actually turn down work if it's not the right "fit" is sage advice for anyone launching or running any kind of business. I can now better understand how Mitch had such an outstanding run with his company. There's much to be learned here!"

– RICK CHUDACOFF, GRAMMY
NOMINATED SONGWRITER & MUSIC
PRODUCER

"I wish I read this book 38 years ago when I opened my business. Read this book and find out why you don't want or need every customer."

– BOB SAVARESE, FOUNDER & PAST
PRESIDENT (MUSIC TRENDS)

"Mitch puts into focus the importance of surrounding yourself with the right clients. After reading *It's The Other Guy* I no longer have to guess who my clients are, and those I want to stay clear of."

–STEVEN METZ, PRESIDENT (CENTRAL
JERSEY POOLS)

"*It's The Other Guy* is an easy and compelling read. Anyone who runs a company, manages a company or is self- employed, should consider this book a "road map" to their business career."

– JEFF MOGIL, CEO (MOGIL ORGANIZATION)

"Mitch Cantor does an excellent job breaking down the complexities of customer interaction in an easy to read entertaining format that is sure to help your bottom line and overall well being."

– PETER LIFRIERI, MARKET RESEARCH AND PRODUCT DEVELOPMENT

IT'S THE OTHER GUY

SAY GOODBYE TO BAD CLIENTS AND HELLO TO BIGGER PROFITS + A BETTER LIFE

MITCH CANTOR

PUBLISHED BY MITCH CANTOR

ISBN 978-1-7334915-0-1 (PAPERBACK)

ISBN 978-1-7334915-1-8 (EPUB)

Special Appreciation for Diane Riis, Earth and Soul Publishing

This book is dedicated with love and thanks to my wife, Marla, and my children Megan and Ryan, who are the most important part of my life. I love each of you to bits. You inspire me and without you, this book and all that's inside it never would have happened.

Marla, you sacrificed so much to allow me to do what I did. I worked long hours and never a complaint from my sweetheart. You truly are my partner, sharing all I went through, advising me with your uncanny feelings about things, and supporting me in every way possible.

Megan and Ryan, you provided me with incentive, drive, and a purpose to succeed. I know I would not have been able to do what I did without my wonderful children.

ACKNOWLEDGMENTS

I'd like to offer my thanks to: *Don Weir* & *Bob Seitz* who were Presidents of Fox Pool Corp during the thirty- five years I was a Fox Pool dealer. Both taught me how to run a better business and I'm forever grateful. Fox Pool Corp was the very best pool company and their product defined the quality I offered. Fox was filled with fantastic people and I don't want to leave anyone out. I'll just say, you provided me immeasurable support. Thank you!

Al Hildebrandt was my General Manager for decades, working tirelessly beside me, and accepting nothing but the best. The successes of my business were largely due to his efforts and for that I am so grateful.

Marty Metz, of Central Jersey Pools had one of the most successful Fox pool franchises and was truly a mentor to me. The year I exceeded his company's annual sales volume was the year I knew my business was truly a success.

Andy Levinson at Jetline Products was my general supplier for decades. Andy would bend over backwards for me – as he did for all his clients. I couldn't have done it without him.

Howie Berger ran Allied Supplies, my main landscaping and patio material supplier. Howie, would go out of his way to get me what I needed as quickly as possible. Howie was the nicest guy, easy to work with, and a tremendously important part of my business.

Diane Riis, my Author's Coach, added a dimension to this work that I am so thankful for. She made my words sound so much more rhythmic, and she is a joy to work with.

Andrea Schmidt, my book designer and book launch helper, was also a pleasure to work with.

CONTENTS

INTRODUCTION

By the time I was ten years old I had my first successful business, snow removal. I was making a couple hundred dollars a day, which was a lot of money for a kid back in the 1960s. I went door to door right after a snow storm, offering to shovel my neighbors' sidewalks and driveways. I was surprised how little competition I had. Pretty soon I had a regular route of customers.

Later on as a teenager on Long Island I landed a job with a small company that installed above-ground swimming pools for people who didn't have the time or ability to install a pool themselves. Once I learned how to do it, I had the confidence to go out on my own. In some ways, my business began at that moment.

Gimbel's department store was a very successful competitor of Macy's, both with flagship stores in New York City. In the basement of my local Gimbel's, there was an array of products such as swing sets, above-ground pools, and the like, all of which you had to install yourself. I presented myself as a full-service installer and gave that department some simple business cards they could hand out to buyers. It was a win/win. Gimbel's sold more product because they could offer an installation alternative, and I was swamped with customers. I kept going. After college I expanded to other retailers who sold, but did not install, above-ground pools.

Since many of those companies didn't need to add an installer to their list, I'd go around their parking lots, putting my business cards under shopper's windshield wipers. I was getting jobs but I wanted the big fish: Harrow's Swimming Pools. It was the largest in the area and is still in business on Long Island. When I got lucky and installed a Harrow's pool, I would ask the home-owners to mention their positive experience with me when they visited the store. It worked and I got on Harrow's installer list. In my first full summer, I had six crews of three people each out installing pools every day.

In a short time, I upgraded to include in-ground swim-ming pools, and formed my company, Sun Design Pools. Later we expanded into custom designed backyard pack-ages including patios, waterfalls, and landscaping. We grew into one of the largest Fox Pool dealers in the country and in 2006 we were awarded a place on the Inc.5000 list as one of the fastest growing small busi-nesses in the country. I ran Sun Design Pools for forty years until I retired.

In-ground swimming pools on Long Island, NY were seasonal and discretionary. Our building season lasted ten months, with some months being very busy, and others slower. People on Long Island use their pools four or five months a year on average, with holidays like Memorial Day and July 4th being "finish line" dates. Though I am writing about conditions as I saw them on the Island, I know you'll find commonalities with your business.

I did a lot of innovation in my day-to-day pool installations because I noticed recurring problems and I created ways to fix them. Over time the features I designed changed how my industry builds pools to this day. If you have a vinyl pool, it's likely you have a feature I innovated. For example, my cantilevered steps and coping are now standard, as are the designs I developed which were manufactured, such as radius corners, that greatly reduced the tendency for the vinyl lining to tear: one of the biggest worries customers always had with vinyl swimming pools.

But, you're not here to learn how to build a better pool. This is a book that can help virtually any business owner, entrepreneur, or salesperson regardless of the price point of your product. My advice can help you as long as WHO your client is matters to you.

This book is the result of experience with many thousands of homeowners I had the pleasure (or displeasure) of working with. In the process of figuring it all out, I worked seven days a week and took calls any time including noon on Sunday from all sorts of customers. The business was my life and I learned a lot, and now, I can share my experience with you and hopefully make your life better.

I believe success and failure really are choices. I assume you are dedicated and willing to put in the work, treat people fairly, and create something you can be proud of. Let me boost those good intentions by sharing the most important thing you need to run a successful business of your own.

1

THE MOST IMPORTANT QUESTION

U sually, if you pick up a book about succeeding in business you will find one of two approaches. One focuses on *how* to do things: how to build, manage, perform, win, and influence so that you can achieve and succeed. The other type of book focuses on *why* you want to do those things in the first place: your mission and core values. "Why" motivates you to get through all the "hows."

Books like "How to Succeed in Business," "How to Win Friends and Influence People," and "How to Grow Your Business Quickly," dominated the store shelves. Actually, you can still find plenty of these kinds of titles, and they're helpful, especially if you don't have a business degree or a successful uncle in the industry to teach you everything he knows.

Finding out "How?" usually costs time and money because you've got to *learn how*. You might spend two or more years earning a degree, getting technical training, or certifications. You could "do your time" under someone's supervision. I wouldn't be surprised if you told me you never have time for books about "how" because you're busy figuring it out on the job.

Knowing "how" eventually makes you an expert in your field, so you can earn more money, climb the corporate ladder, or go out on your own. If you rack up some years of experience and do really well, or if you develop some special method, you can write a book about your "how" and make some passive income sharing what you learned through years of trial and error.

I'm going to assume you either know how to run your business, or, you can find what you need to know. If you've got the hows down and your business is still not as successful as you want, then you might ask yourself another question: Why?

WHY?

Leadership guru Simon Sinek is famous for advising us to "Start with why." The thinking goes, with a strong enough mission, inner fire, and clear vision you can always achieve your "how." I agree we need it, because the "hows" of running a successful business are time-consuming, challenging, even grueling. "How?" always requires persistence, refinement, and effort because "how?" is about methods, and methods don't always work.

Asking "why?" is about drilling down, going deeper; and possibly gathering your team for visioning processes with a coach or consultant. I actually did a lot of that sort of thing myself with my people. Nobody could motivate my employees better than me!

Knowing why can enhance your business and your life. But you can be highly motivated and certain of your values, and still not achieve the success you deserve.

So, let me add another question into the mix.

WHO?

Your success doesn't only hinge on knowing your industry, training to be the best in your field, or letting your deep "why?" motivate you. When the day-to-day push comes to shove, *who* you work with (and for) is as important as all the rest. Who you serve, and whether or not you are a good match has so much to do with your success. "Who?" is the subject of this book because *if you're only asking "How?" or "Why?" you're missing an important question.*

If you need to be in a relationship with your customers for weeks, months, or even years, you really need to figure out the "who?" question. If you are a business owner, like a contractor, coach, real estate agent, web designer, or wedding planner; if you work one-on-one with clients and you have some control over who you choose to work with, then "who?" matters a great deal. In fact, if common wisdom is correct and we are the sum total of who we surround ourselves with, "who?" shapes more than just your business. It affects your entire life and even who YOU become.

2

IT'S NOT YOU

About twenty years ago I was building a pool for the Brills in Bellmore. They lived on a curving road so you couldn't see their house until just before you turned down the street. Before I started the job, I had a twenty-yard dumpster delivered to the curb in front of the house. The dumpster had reflectors on it, and in my opinion wasn't in a dangerous location, but the Brills were worried that someone wouldn't see it in the evening and would drive into it.

I was just starting to build a relationship with them so fluffing off their concern wasn't an option. Assuring the homeowner nothing bad would happen wasn't enough. I had to get creative. It was December and getting dark by 5:00pm. So, I picked up a few boxes of Christmas lights and I strung them on the dumpster. Once it was lit up, no driver could possibly miss it. Now the neighborhood had some holiday cheer and the Brills' safety concerns were handled. They were ecstatic and I'd powerfully turned a worry into a positive at a very low cost to me.

Most important, I showed my customers how I would deal with any future issues: I'd take them seriously, and I'd be creative. Their confidence in me went through the roof. Over the years many of my best referrals came from this family.

The dumpster was my version of turning lemons into lemonade. You can find dumpster ideas of your own – ways you can turn a potential disaster into loyalty and referrals for your business. Embrace your problems because they can become very positive experiences for you and your clients. *With one big caveat.*

It's Not You, It's the Other Guy

I realized that finding creative answers to the smallest issues was *the* way to build a more rewarding relationship with my customers. In fact, early on I started to look for small concerns I could handle to show my attention to detail, and my desire to be the best in the business. I taught my employees the same thing: that everything matters, no matter how insignificant it seemed. But, over time I discovered that even this level of commitment to customer satisfaction could only go so far. The Brills loved the dumpster solution but not everybody would have. In fact, some people might even have been offended. Eventually it dawned on me: even my best, most creative efforts to add safety, value, and satisfaction to the job only mattered to the "right" customer. This is why I can tell you, if you're not working with the right people, all your efforts are for nothing.

You've probably been told a thousand times that you have to beat the competition, innovate, develop a plat-form. You probably think you need more training, better staff, and better marketing. I'm here to say you may not need any of those things. In fact, if you've been struggling, it may not be your fault – and there's nothing to change except for one small, very significant thing, which you can do immediately. Put this into practice and watch what happens to your business and your life.

That universal WHO is the focus of this book. Since I didn't want to overload you with swimming pool examples, I reached out to friends who are in business for themselves. They've given me permission to share their experiences with the clients they've come across over the years. I am sure between all of us, you'll see some of your own clients in our stories. We can help you map your way out and around the people who don't contribute to your success, but who drag you down instead.

Advice for the Sale and Beyond

I evaluated every job, whether it was installing a pool or signing a service contract or even the one-off emergency response requests with one guiding question was: would this customer contribute to my success and overall happiness, or would they be a drain on me, my staff, and my resources? The answer was crucial to all aspects of my business and the same is true for you. It's a long view, but if you take it, you'll see an improvement in your business right now and over time.

Naturally, in any business, the offer and negotiation are key. Without the sale, you're out of business. But whether you price the job too high, too low, or just right, if it's the *wrong customer* you cannot win. If you agree to work with difficult people who are only concerned about the money they've spent, they will be back in your office or showroom with a thousand complaints or you'll be running back to their house time and time again to fix many (often imaginary) problems. If you opt to sign a nitpicker, any little glitch along the way, whether it's a delay or something that doesn't meet their expectations, will have you jumping. That's stressful for your team and for you. But even worse, in the end, you will find yourself losing money and adding aggravation. So, more important than the sales price, your work ethic, and your careful attention to detail, there is one thing that can make or break you: the customer you choose to work *with*.

I wanted to work with a certain type of customer because I knew I'd be interacting with them for months and even years, since in addition to new pool installations, we offered all services, including upkeep and emergency visits as well. Making a mistake at the time of the sale or enrollment can make you miserable for a good, long time.

A friend of mine, Rick, is a contractor who was referred to Catalina, who wanted an extensive renovation of her kitchen and living area. It was the kind of project that involved numerous subcontractors, inevitable wait-times for things like granite counters, custom cabinetry, and the like. Rick would be in and out of Catalina's home for a long time. She had high standards, but Rick was used to meeting those. As the project wore on, however, Catalina went from demanding to impossible. By the end of the job she complained about everything, did research on YouTube so she could tell the plumber how it *should* be done, and stood over Rick, telling him exactly how many nails to use in her crown molding. She threw workers out of her house regularly. She made a nasty call to Rick at the end of many days. If you asked him, Rick would tell you that while he did make money, the job was not worth the aggravation.

The One Who Got Away

Have you ever had a lead you wished you'd let go? Anyone who became a customer you'd have been better off without? I'm going to bet that if you've been in business for any length of time, the answer is "yes," and you probably first realized it in the middle of some sleepless night, when you couldn't stop the angry or anxious thoughts racing around your head. That's a symptom of a job you should've passed on.

You might be skeptical. Aren't you supposed to make every sale you can? Isn't everyone a potential customer, at least within your niche? What about when you're starting out? Isn't the frustration of a difficult customer worth it to build up your business? No. I learned to go into every sales call with the idea that there are sales I would be better off not making.

Another friend, Larry, who owns a construction company, gave me a prime example. From the moment Larry walked into this particular prospect's home, he knew something was off. When he spoke with the woman and her son, his suspicion was confirmed. They told him how they'd just sued one contractor, thrown another off the job, and how a third walked away in the middle of the project. It wasn't hard for Larry to walk away too and not even start the project.

Donna, a friend who is a coach, was looking to grow her

practice and had a prospect she'd spoken to a number of times. Donna doubted whether they were a match but she didn't think she could afford to turn down a client. But every call seemed to focus on overcoming sales resistance and negativity. In her gut, Donna knew working with this woman would be an uphill battle. She decided there was no joy in that kind of relationship and let go to make room for others who would be happy to invest in coaching with her.

In the end, I can't convince you to pass up the customers who will make your life difficult, but I can prepare you for what you're getting yourself into. After a while, you'll see the wisdom in trimming your clientele to those who are going to give you satisfaction, healthy profit, and high morale among your team. In other words, you'll come to appreciate that there are customers who make it worth your while, and others who will have a crushing impact on everything you do.

3

THE THING NO ONE IS TALKING
ABOUT

I f you wonder why every client encounter is a grind, you are swamped with complaints, unpaid balances, and unhappy customers, then I am about to give you a big sense of relief. It's not you. It's the other guy. Nobody is saying that, and maybe it's politically incorrect. But once you identify *who* the problem is, you will turn your whole business life around. I don't mean you should start discriminating against anyone because of their race, gender, or political affiliation. I am talking about screening out the troublemakers who can make your life miserable because of their attitude *toward you*.

There are three types of customers you are going to meet in your business and unless you know who you are dealing with, it will cost you time, money, and aggravation. Who you agree to work with is as important as any other single thing you do on the job site or in your business. How to figure out the best match and build rapport

22

with an ideal client is the key to your success and to real satisfaction in your business life.

Screen out the Heart-Breakers

Look at it this way: we all have relatives we love and relatives we put up with. Think about a family function with only the ones you love versus an event that includes the ones you tolerate. It's a whole different experience: much less fun, creative, easy, and enjoyable. You can't choose your relatives but fortunately, you can choose your customers.

Learn how to screen out the heart-breakers and watch your enjoyment, reputation, work-life balance, success, and even your worker-retention soar. When the frustration caused by the worst clients is off your plate, you'll have time to dedicate to the people who make you the most money and bring the greatest satisfaction and the best referrals over the long haul.

You may be able to recognize the "wrong" customer instantly, but I didn't. That's why I am suggesting that you go into every interaction expecting to meet the best client you ever worked for. Until they prove you wrong, you are about to sign the #1 client, your dream customer. Get prepared to meet them at that level of expectation. Get ready to serve them to the highest degree.

I would bring my A game and focus on building rapport before presenting an offer or even starting a discussion of the product. Until I had rapport, I would never even use the word "pool." Let it take some time. The process of rapport-building can tell you a lot about the prospect, and that is quality time you want to spend. Ask questions, be observant. Do you feel a kinship with them? Do you have anything in common? Does it feel like you can communicate easily? What does your gut tell you?

I got to the point where I knew right away when something was off. Eventually, I got to the *next* point, which was doing something about my hunch! So, even though the sale was in hand, if it was not right, I would turn it down. Knowing when to do that became more important than the sales I actually closed.

Recently at an open house, a newbie realtor folded up the sign-in sheet and handed it to the long-term professional agent who had held the open house.

"Do you follow up with everyone who signs in?" he asked her.

"No, not everyone."

"OK, so how do you know who to follow up on?"

She smiled and said, "Well, I'm getting a little jaded. But now I only follow up on the people I want to work with. There are some people you know are "your people." Walking them through the house I get a gut feeling that I can have a good relationship with them. We smile, we laugh, and I know it's something I want to do."

Even though she is selective, she is a very successful agent. Not following up on every single lead has not gotten in her way, it has made her life easier and her business profitable. Think of all the time she isn't wasting trying to communicate with a client who doesn't "get" her style or her personality. Think about all the time she saves not trying to do the impossible, schmoozing just to create a client. Some people just aren't the right fit. Not for her, and not for you. The successful realtor just goes toward the people she fits with.

A few things might come up for you. Will you learn to recognize the wrong customer? Yes, as you go through your rapport-building time. You will get to know them, listen to what they want, and soon you will have a sense whether this is a match or not. But we will get more specific about how you figure out who those great (and not so great) prospects are.

Another thing you might be wondering is how to let someone go if you decide you don't want to work with them. I find the easiest way is to give them your list price and stay firm on it. The troubling customers will not pay list price.

Finally, even if you go in hoping to say an enthusiastic "yes!" to your prospect, you've got to be OK saying "no" to some customers no matter how much you want the business. The first time I realized this was many years ago. I was with some people who were pushing on price. I knew if I agreed, I could not deliver the quality of product I prided myself on. They were asking for too much for the price. But it was more than that: everything seemed wrong. You will come to find the same thing. It seems like a prospect is hung up on price, but if you scratch the surface, you'll find someone who won't be satisfied no matter how cheap you go.

In any case, I didn't get the job. Six months later I was talking to a friendly competitor and these people came up for some reason. Turns out, this other company built a pool for them and the experience was just terrible. The other company was in the process of suing them to get paid! I dodged a bullet. At that moment I realized how important it was to trust my gut and walk away.

I have found that when I didn't waste time with the wrong people, I was more creative. I had the chance to think, to solve problems, work on insights about innovations, and daydream about the future. You'll be surprised what happens when your day isn't taken up with putting out fires on every job site you have going. You will have more time to work with the right customers and grow your business.

Not My Problem

Another feature of businesses like mine has to do with the sales team. If your salespeople are only involved in the initial sale and aren't required to see the customer again, you've got to incentivize them to care about attracting and signing the right customer – and to let a sale go if it isn't. If they make the sale, get the commission and move on, they have zero incentive to walk away from the people who will drive the rest of you crazy. I used to handle it this way: make it mandatory that the salesperson keeps in touch and stays involved with the entire installation and delivery of the product. If your salespeople are going to have a relationship with the customer throughout the whole process, they will understand – and fast – how important signing the right customer is. With that realization, they no longer want the sale at any cost and they stop signing up people who will make them miserable for months. If you have a sales team that doesn't understand the pressure and angst a difficult customer can bring, the owner or manager has to incentivize the salesperson to care.

Another way I solved the salesperson problem was that all of my salespeople had other positions within the company. One was the construction manager; another was sales manager; and another was an office staffer. I never used a completely outside salesperson. An advantage was my team member could tell the customer they wouldn't just sign the deal and never be seen again. Instead, this employee could honestly claim they'd be involved with the whole project from start to finish. Clients loved to hear this as they'd often bond with the salesperson and now, they knew the person they trusted would have their back through the whole process. It was a win-win all around.

To Be or Not

Does the idea that you can *let* a potential client become part of your customer base sound backward? Shouldn't you be doing your utmost to get the customers to pick *you?* This is not a one-way street, and they are not only shopping YOU. You are very definitely screening them as well.

If you can figure out whether the potential client would be fair, helpful, and considerate; if you could tell they'd never try to take undue advantage of you, you'd want to work with them. But, on the other hand, if you meet a client who always wants more for less; if they act hostile or complain from the very start, you should think twice about working with them. So, how can you tell for sure?

So, Who Are We Dealing With?

Here's a quick overview:

Your # 1 customer is demanding. I'm going to call them the "Elite." He or she wants the best from you (and everybody else,) and is not looking for any problems – they will expect *you* to see to that. In other words, they want to make sure your whole operation is glitch-free. They will pay list price (or close,) make payments on time, and be realistic about the schedule – though once you set the schedule, you'd better be ready to stick to it. Although they are demanding, they are fair; they are exacting but don't expect the impossible. They won't cause aggravation for you and your employees and they won't tolerate any either.

The second type of customer wrestles somewhat for a discount, but gives back in so many ways. They are "Fair and Flexible." You'll find the flexibility in scheduling and adapting to adjustments in the agreement you made. They will allow for delays and be understanding if you must add on to the project. For example, if you're a contractor you never know what you're going to find if you open up a bathroom wall. There might be mold from an undetected leak. There might be inadequate floor support for the claw foot tub. Explaining the additional time and money to a Fair and Flexible client will not drive your job off the rails.

This type of client will often be an active part of the job. They might actually be helpful – I used to joke that if you let them, they'd jump in and help dig the hole. They will pay you on time and are pleasant to work with. Their interest and involvement in the job, and their easy-going attitude and flexibility when there are problems, will make you want to give them 110% effort. These are the clients who can make doing the job fun.

The dreaded #3 customer, who I will call the "Red Flag," is a total pain in the butt. They bargain you down hard, while promising to be easy to work with. Once the job starts you quickly find out they are anything but easy. In fact, everything is a giant problem, even when there is no problem at all. You'll find it hard to get paid, and you will regret any concessions you made on price. You will wish there was an aggravation surcharge to put on jobs like this one. Don't worry though, the Red Flag prospects send up red flags. If you're watching for them, you can avoid going down a bumpy road.

I'm Going to Save You Some Time

It took time for me to figure out who was who. At first it was not obvious. Sure, I remember the times when I knew from the moment I walked through the door that a client was not for me. For example, early on I figured out that if a prospect complained about another contractor, it was only a matter of time before they'd be complaining about me. I learned that people will give themselves away. For example, someone who tells you, "I've never had a person work in this house who didn't try to rip me off," is a client who will probably accuse you of ripping them off!

Sometimes I'd see how rude the prospects could be to their family members, creating a toxic atmosphere I knew would eventually extend to me too. It was a definite red flag if someone thought all of my prices were ridiculous no matter what I offered. In these cases, I learned not to budge on my list-price proposal. Most Red Flags turn that offer down, and I would never look back.

Some people are obviously wrong for you, but it takes time to learn the fakers.

You might meet someone and you think how nice they are, how friendly they are, and how easy they will be to work with. It's not always your misread that gets you into trouble. Some people actively try to fool you. It's part of their deal negotiation. There are also people who change their spots once a deal is signed. The nice guy is gone and the problems start. It's as if once you agreed to work for them, the power dynamic changes. You are no longer their equal, but instead, their underling. Now you work for them and they are in control.

Once I figured out who to avoid, my entire life changed. I used to feel obligated to work with anyone who wanted to hire me – but I wasn't – and neither are you.

4

RAPPORT

Y ou are about to walk into someone's house and sell them a high-ticket item. If you go in feeling like you have a gift to give to them, something they will get value from and treasure for years to come, you are pretty confident that you can make the sale. But, by now you know I don't think that's always the most important consideration. Are you as confident this is the type of customer you want to sign? Will you love working with this person for the long haul? Will your employees wind up hating you for signing them?

Who's Choosing Who?

When you go on a sales call, you are not the only person in the hot seat. Shift your thinking about being at the mercy of your prospects. Your business does not hinge on whether this particular person agrees to work with you or not. What would be different if you went into your sales meetings with that attitude?

How often does a consumer think they're going to potentially be rejected by the contractor who is estimating their job? Not often. That gives you an advantage. Your prospect doesn't realize it, but you are trying to decide if they're right for you too. What you decide will either save you from some miserable months or create a client who is a joy to work with and who refers you to their wonderful friends and co-workers for years.

A Friend for Life

Figuring out the right client is mostly a gut thing. With the right person you will feel something like an attraction or affinity. Maybe the best word is chemistry, which is hard to define. I don't have a checklist per se: unless a prospect has certain characteristics, you say goodbye. But, if you know what it feels like to have chemistry with someone, you can learn to trust it, and let it lead you. You can figure out in a short time if they're right for you. The question I asked myself is whether or not I'd be friends with this individual. My goal was to make all my clients my friends, and for the most part, I was able to – which isn't to say I wanted to hang out every weekend. It meant I was looking for a certain amount of warmth, familiarity, and friendliness between us.

Building Friendly Rapport

If you are meeting someone at a social event for the first time, you'd ask about their interests, their job, or their family. You'd look for things you might have in common, to make conversation and connection easier. Rapport-building with a client works the same way.

I used to walk into a prospective customer's home and look around for things we had in common. For example, if that classic picture of a child in a Little League uniform was hanging on the wall, I would talk about my own child's Little League and how I used to be a coach. I would compliment things that looked nice, and most of all I'd listen to what my hosts said. What were their concerns; what did they value?

When you have real rapport, you'll find it much easier to be in charge of the conversation. This isn't to say you should dominate or control the conversation. What I mean is your prospect will allow you to be the guide because you've established trust and credibility.

When you are in rapport with someone, you are not just panting, waiting for them to say, "yes, I want to hire you." You are in a conversation, even though it's one with a clear goal in mind. You are taking your time, going slowly, back and forth the way you would talk to a friend. And, you are being an active player in the relationship that you are going to develop.

If you go into someone's home and you're trying to build rapport and they are trying to build rapport back, that's a very good sign. They care about the relationship as much as you do. Not only are they listening to your pitch – which cannot come before rapport is established – they want to know whether you're a nice person, whether you'll be easy to work with, accommodating, flexible – exactly what you want to know about them. Just as you don't want to take advantage, neither do they. You both want to create a give and take. You can feel it when someone is leaning toward you, making an effort to get to know you. You'll see it in their body language –

they might *literally* lean toward you, look you in the eye, nod and laugh at the right places. They know you're trying to break the ice and show who you are, not only trying to make a sale.

There are people who don't respond to your overtures. You can feel their defensiveness – as if they are just waiting to be taken advantage of or, are ready to pounce to take advantage of you. So, watch what happens when you arrive at their house. Is there chemistry? How do they treat you? Do they offer you a cup of coffee? Do they make pleasant chit-chat or do they seem suspicious? Listen to your gut. Do you feel like something is off? You can sit at their table and know in 15 minutes if you would go out to dinner with them and have a good time. As you are trying to make a personal connection, do they interrupt by saying, "Let's get down to what it costs." If they don't care to make you their friend, that tells you a lot.

Granted, there are people who don't do "small talk." They are all business and that's OK. They can still become some of your best clients. As long as they treat you respectfully and hear you out, and they aren't giving off warning signals by kicking the cat or rudely taking phone calls during your appointment, you can assume they are a good prospect. Honor their time by not going overboard trying to win them over. Match their attitude. Give them what they are looking for, be direct and polite. Once an "all business" client makes the decision to hire you, the walls may come down.

I became friends with "Elite" clients Wayne and Audrey Sosin. I will tell you more about them in the next chapter. For now I will say that what impressed me was how they showed me they cared about me as a person. They always offered me a drink and made me feel at home. I knew I was in the right place when they introduced me to the family. I was treated like a guest in their home instead of just a hired hand who they could ignore. It's something to watch for: if a prospect doesn't stop and introduce you when a family member walks in the room, that could be a red flag.

Nobody's for Everybody

When you are building a business one of the things you learn is to "niche" yourself. That means identifying your likely customers, whether it's geographically, demographically or according to the product or service you offer. Until you have your niche nailed down, you'll be tempted to target *everyone* who crosses your path. But, you're not the right match for everyone – and more important – not everyone is right for you, either.

You work hard, putting in your long days, seven days a week, especially at the beginning, and you are learning how to manage time and run things more efficiently. Maybe you think you can handle the drain on your time and resources that a Red Flag can bring. Maybe you figure everyone gets that stinky customer. "Oh, I'll deal with it, I can't give away a sale." But you only have a certain number of hours in your week and you don't want to waste them getting pulled away constantly with irrational demands from one or two Red Flag customers. You don't want to lose a great job because you're too busy or preoccupied with a troublesome one. Don't let your need, fear, inexperience, or what someone else taught you about never passing up a sale, prevent you from saying "no" when your gut tells you to. If you wouldn't be friends with a prospect, you may not want to work with them either.

The impact of a no-win customer also creates negativity for your employees, which drains their energy and enthusiasm. You want to build an environment where everyone is happy to come in to work and purposefully do their job, making your customers happy. When every body is miserable, no matter what you do, the client is miserable too. And that is not the message you want them to spread about you. Let them spread it about your competition!

Sending in the Team

If you are a business owner who sends a salesperson into the field, as I mentioned, keep them in touch with the clients they signed. It's the best way to show them that not every client is worth the sale. Early in my business, before I realized I was going to have to train salespeople to see prospects the way I did, they would sell a job and not give a second thought to what the clients might be like to work for. To them, the job was so big, and the commission was so great, that they didn't care whether the person was right for us or not. I found ways to keep the salespeople active with customers, and once they had to follow up on calls and complaints they'd say, "Wow, that one pool drove me nuts!"

People who were Red Flags often got attached to their salespeople though, which I thought was interesting. Sometimes, after the pool was finished and there were things they didn't like, even though I wasn't involved in their choices, they still saw me as the bad guy. As far as they were concerned, the salesperson was on their side. Even if the salesperson told them not to do something and they went ahead, or he or she sold something they shouldn't have, they were never to blame – I was. The Red Flag would come complaining to me, but their loyalty would still be to the salesperson. The customer perceived me, the owner, as rich; that my only incentive was to make a profit, to provide cheap goods at a high price, which was never the case at all.

This is not to say the sales team was at fault – they just hadn't been educated in recognizing the types of customers, or they felt it was important to land every single client they could. Over time, they found that wasn't my goal for them at all. I wanted our entire team experience to be positive and the process of signing the right customers was key.

About Sales and Staff

One way to insure a more enjoyable work life is to only hire nice people to work for you. With staff you have a lot more control – the ultimate control! I wanted to create a family atmosphere and go beyond just liking the people who worked for me. When I was hiring employees the most important qualification was that they be a nice person. I figured I could train a decent person to be a good mechanic, but I could not teach a talented mechanic how to be nice. I wanted to be able to tell clients that they would like everyone who walked into their backyard, and in order for that to be true I had to feel that way myself. My advice is always to hire the right people and treat them well – not just fairly – treat them the best.

I was clear with my employees that I wanted them to be polite, neat, and caring on the job. I wanted them to care about the homeowner and the property, and to take pride in their work. I asked them to wear company shirts and jackets, because I didn't like the ragged appearance of workers in ripped tee shirts, and because I believed in the power of logos and putting the name of the business on the shirt.

Why YOUR Happiness Matters

I believe when the boss is happy, it trickles down. Employees feel it and you start to pick up clients who are a joy and not a drag to work with. The team has less stress all day and they start seeing you as the person who has stepped up to protect them from the people who will make them miserable. You become the hero, they work happier, you get more productivity in the office, on the sales front, and on the job. The value of your staff goes up, and frankly, your stock has gone up in their eyes, too. Now everyone is getting along – from customers to staff to you. And that's a happy business!

Screening Tools

I mentioned that I was very big on home shows. I would always take three or four employees with me because home shows are a winter project, and it was a productive way to keep my people busy in the off season. Shoppers would get to meet my key people: the service or office manager, for example. These would be people they'd be interacting with a lot in the short, and ideally, the long term, as we would maintain the contract to service, open, and close their pool each year. At the booth it was all about building rapport, not showing shoppers our pools, but meeting me, and meeting the team.

I used to do "meet and greets" at people's homes while I was building their pool and after. I'd come over with hotdogs and I'd meet the neighbors that way. Get social with your prospects and see if you can forge a relationship with some of them. Not only will you get more business but you'll have a better handle on who you want to work with and who you'd be better off passing on. One friend and business owner attended her town's annual expo and she actually took notes on the people who came to her table, to remind herself who she clicked with and wanted to follow up on.

Visibility

Of course, without access to prospects you will never get the chance to choose who you work with. Visibility includes things like signing up for home shows and expos and other techniques as well. I used to put permanent stickers with my name and phone number on pool filters so that when the house was sold, the new owner would know who to call for service. I was big on job site signs and any way I could advertise on the block I was working on. Our trucks were neatly lettered with our contact information. I wanted to let the neighbors know we were there. Sometimes I would go up and down the block when I was building a new pool telling people, "Feel free to stop by!" I was trying to build relationships with the neighbors, one of the best places to secure new jobs – and it worked. Sometimes I would get three or four pools on the block. But the key was the face to face contact. The neighbors could see what I was all about, but I could also check them out. I was getting social, and it was better than anything else out there, including Facebook.

Chapter Takeaway

What is the equivalent of a home show for you? How can you get out and be among your prospects face to face?

5

THE ELITE

The #1 type of customer is the "Elite," the cream of the crop. When you come across them, you cherish them. The rewards of working with an Elite are huge, both financially and emotionally. But you must produce the goods. By "the goods", I mean being the best company you can be – on all levels. Nothing is too good for the Elite. From the first contact to the close of the project you have to be mindful of every step. Skimping on quality product or materials will not be tolerated, neither will slip-ups in workmanship, or missed milestones. They expect you to return their calls in a reasonable amount of time, meet your agreed-upon deadlines, and be considerate of their home and property. They expect the highest quality workmanship and products. They are willing to pay list price but will settle for nothing less than excellence from you. If you provide 5-star service, you will be rewarded.

I found it was more than top quality and the most up-to-date product and technology they wanted. They wanted nice people working around their homes. At the end of the day what I realized was they weren't paying just for the pool. They were paying for US.

How Do You Recognize an Elite Customer?

How will you know you've just driven up to the house of an Elite client? They surround themselves with quality – but not necessarily luxury. Keep that in mind. They are not necessarily the richest of your prospects.

Check out their car, their landscaping, the town they live in. These things are signs they could be Elites. Wealth and being demanding (or maybe I should say exacting) often go hand in hand, but this isn't to say that all Elites are well-off. Some people just set aside money for the things that mean a great deal to them, and if it is their home (or the product that they are buying from you), they want the best. Maybe they've saved for it, or have dreamed of it for years, but if the time has come for them to do the project or make the purchase, they are willing to do it right and spend whatever it costs to get it done. So, you have to meet them where they are. They are expecting exceptional quality and you have to deliver it.

You cannot have the success you crave with the #1 customer if you're not the cream of the crop yourself. Maybe you're not the most expensive or well-known, but you better have something amazing that sets you apart and makes you the best. The #1 customer who is sending you "buy" signals needs to hear you say you are the top of the line so step up and say it, then do your best to exceed their expectations.

The Elite Customer is not going to accept inferior products and you're going to have to abandon short cuts. This was key to working with Elite customers who will pay more for excellence, experience, and expertise.

Clearly, I am not writing for the "low-ball" type of business owner here. If you want the kind of success I enjoyed, you have to go after the top of the line customer, and then show up as the top provider in your industry. Then, you've got to build it the same as you would for yourself, maybe even better.

Expectation is Everything

I tried to continually make my company Elite-level. My products were the highest quality and I didn't avoid talking about that in my literature and presentations. We preached the importance of EXCELLENCE instead of emphasizing price. We were singing to the Elites.

Years ago, I read an article in Newsday, the primary newspaper on Long Island, about succeeding in business. It advised being "the best" and structuring your prices to reflect the extra costs of being the best. The writer recommended adding a reasonable premium on top of the normal mark-up. He said that being the best put you in a class by yourself, and afforded you the privilege of charging for it. I took it to mean if you want an "Elite" clientele, you have to be an elite business owner.

Over the years I heard business owners complain that they couldn't afford to provide a client with the service they demand – they couldn't afford their ideal client! It sounds crazy but it goes back to that Newsday article that said you've got to cover the cost of being the best.

The solution: ask for what it costs to provide the level of service you want to offer and never be afraid to be among the higher priced. If you start lower in order to get the job, but then are unable to cover your costs, the resentment it can potentially generate in you can lead to skimping on quality or taking short-cuts, which will be devastating to the relationship you are trying to build. Especially when it comes to the Elite customer, where cutting corners will not go unnoticed. Is it worth it?

I can virtually guarantee you that everyone has to resist the temptation to charge less, bargain, discount their services, or use inferior product, equipment, or technology. Don't do it. Abandon the shortcut, don't barter on price (or at least don't make it the central part of your discussion), create a referral-worthy product, and watch your business grow as a result.

Elite customers aren't unreasonable. They are not looking for you to go to the moon. They just want you to exceed their expectations – and that doesn't have to cost a cent. Stay in rapport, be in regular contact with them about the job, do your best work, and you'll find this is the most profitable of all your clients.

Your biggest confirmation that you've found an Elite prospect comes when you negotiate the price. An Elite Customer does not haggle. They may ask whether the price you quoted is your best one, but they will not fight you for a lower price. They don't want to spend more than they have to, but they are willing to spend to get exactly what they want. You might want to say something like, "I know you won't be happy unless we install the most amazing pool and to do that, I have to charge you a fair price."

I am not saying that haggling on the price means someone won't be great to work with, but they are not an Elite by definition.

Your Work Isn't Over Once You Get the Job

You will have to continue to prove yourself to an Elite, even after they hire you. I worked with Wayne and Audrey Sosin in Woodbury. They looked for the best and when they hired me, I knew I was on "probation." After a week or so, they got to know me. They saw I made the right decisions and they stopped questioning me so closely. They learned to trust me and once that happened, they put the ball in my court. Once I'd proven myself, I never again felt like they were watching over me. They knew I was going to manage the project as I'd promised and I'd pay attention to all the little details that it would be easy to forget about. I got many quality recommendations from this couple. They told me I was one of the very few contractors they would ever recommend. Referrals like the ones I got from the Sosins prove the value of your Elite customer goes way beyond your time on their particular job.

Elite customers will pay you on time, and they won't hold out over issues or complain about insignificant things. If you've built rapport with this type of client, they will trust that by the end of the job you will have taken care of the small things that maybe they did notice, but never commented on. They are willing to wait for the "wow." Finally, at the end of the job and going forward for (ideally) years, they will recommend you to their friends and neighbors.

I walked into every presentation expecting an Elite

customer. Until I was proven wrong, I assumed everyone was going to be a #1 just in case I was about to meet a unique and valuable prospect, who would bring the best out of me, and pay top dollar for my services.

The Elite clients will pave the way to a very successful business. Unfortunately, they are a distinct minority. Just like celebrities in expensive gowns striding down the red carpet, the #1 customer is a bit of celebrity in the business world and they don't stroll along every day. As a sales person or a business owner, you know the thrill of seeing someone who may be like that walking into your showroom or your home show booth. You know right off the bat you have someone willing to pay top dollar to get the best. What do you do when you cross paths with that prospect? What will keep them from passing you by? How do you hook them and more importantly convince them that your standards will meet theirs?

1. Look the part. Smile. Put your best foot forward in terms of appearance and attitude. That means being a friendly professional. Dress appropriately for your market and your industry. As you know I was big into company shirts and jackets. I flooded my employees with clothing. I used to see other companies go out in torn tee shirts, and it looked ragged. I felt dressing nicely, with the business name and logo displayed proudly at all times, showed something about the company.

2. Build rapport. Show them immediately what it will be like to work with you. Pay a simple compliment, show interest beyond the sale.

Look for things you have in common to build a connection. Listen to their concerns.

3. Have high-quality literature to leave with your prospect. Make it helpful, informative, and valuable. Refer them to your excellent, professionally built website and numerous positive reviews. Give them the phone numbers of people they can call who already love you.

4. Work with established firms. Show your client you are like them in that you only buy the best. For example, I only sold Fox Pools because I knew they were the top of the line. They cost more, but I wanted to be able to offer that level of quality to my customers, whether they knew Fox Pool's reputation or not.

5. Talk quality, not price, from start to finish.

Let Your High-End Lift You

If you are lucky enough to sign an Elite but don't feel like you're the best in your field, you better find a way to get there. I bet you already know what your weak spots are. Maybe it's a lagging employee or a supplier that doesn't always come up to your standards. Now is the time to clean that up. Let your Elite customers challenge you to up-level your products and services. Let them make you better. They will teach you so much about how to keep all of your customers happy going forward.

Paying for the Privilege

From the very first meeting, all the way through to the end and even beyond, you have to put the Elite jobs as first priority. They are paying for that privilege. Concentrate on making them feel special at all times. The rewards are many because an Elite is generally a successful person and they will help you be more successful too. They will make you so happy you found them.

One of the great rewards of working with an Elite will be those referrals they deliver to you. I remember getting calls from referred clients who would say, "If you could make my friend happy, you can make *anyone* happy!"

Obviously, not every client is going to be an Elite, and that's not all bad news. Some of my favorite clients, probably the easiest to deal with, weren't Elite, but were in the next category – the "Fair and Flexible," the type of client that made my day easier every chance they got.

Chapter Takeaway

Elite customers:

1. Demand the best and can bring the best out in you.

2. Do not haggle over price and pay in full, on time.

3. Are willing to wait for the "wow."

6

FAIR AND FLEXIBLE

I built two pools for Bob and Holly Savarese. They were among the nicest clients to work with. They would always ask for a small discount – in fact, Bob would bargain at every add-on, but then we'd laugh about it. He would also help me, for example by turning the water off himself when the pool was first filling instead of making us run back over to his house later to do it. Bob would move my company's job site sign around the property to show it off to its best advantage. He and Holly would talk to their neighbors about me, and I wound up doing their next-door neighbor's pool based on Bob and Holly's recommendation. The pool was sold before I walked in because of how Bob spoke about us.

The Savareses were known to treat my guys to lunch, which saved time running out to delis, and shaved time off the job, though I doubt they did it for that reason. Everybody on my team wanted to go there because the Savareses treated them so nicely. The friendly "fight" to be going to the Savarese's each day was a fun and beautiful aspect of the morning. They were easy to deal with, always paid me quickly, and provided me tons of recommendations. This family is a great example of Fair and Flexible client, the kind that you will be fortunate to work with.

Who is Fair and Flexible?

If I met a prospective Fair and Flexible client who I knew I'd enjoy working with, I would make sure they'd become one of my customers. Honestly, I would have felt bad if these nice people used one of those jerks out there! I would basically tell them, "Nobody is going to do the job I will do for you." It wasn't even a price thing; it was the experience they were going to have – and I wanted to be able to deliver it.

When you go to the home of a Fair and Flexible prospect, you'll find rapport building relatively easy. That's because they are generally warm and open – it's who they are: nice people! They are considerate from the start; they thank you for spending time with them.

See what you notice when you listen to them. Fair and Flexible people speak kindly of other contractors and are courteous to visitors who may be in the house when you are working there. Most of all, they are nice to their children. I believe people show you who they are in the way they treat their kids. Does the customer say, "Leave us alone!" and send the kids out of the room? Or do they introduce you to the kids, as if they – and you – matter? People should love their kids more than anything else in the world, and if they don't treat them nicely, they won't treat you nicely either.

No matter how the family seems when you walk in and meet everyone, no matter how confident you are that you will make the sale, wait until you feel a level of comfort, even a feeling of friendship, before you begin to talk about your product. Don't rush the rapport building, even if you feel it is going extremely well.

Just because everyone is being very agreeable, when it comes time to mention the prices, there will be negotiation. Give and take is a characteristic of your interaction with Fair and Flexible client. Don't be put off or think you've sized them up wrong. If you tell them what you want, they will tell you what they want, and you'll land in a place where everyone's happy. Being easy-going is one of their characteristics, but that doesn't mean they accept your first quote without a question.

Fair and Flexible clients go into the conversation aware that they get what they pay for. They understand it is a mutual deal: they are seeking something and so are you. Don't be put off by the request for a better price. You know what you need to make on the job. Let compromise lead the discussion from there. They will appreciate your willingness to negotiate. You may settle on a lower price point but it will be worth it because your time with Fair and Flexible customers will be among the highlights of your season – that was definitely true for me.

Once you have come to an agreement and you start the job, you'll find that scheduling is easier with a Fair and Flexible client. If it rained for a week in the end of June and you're not getting that pool finished by the all-important deadline of July 4th, this client will understand. If you have to delay the start of a job, they will take it in stride. They will not become irrationally angry if rainy weather makes the ground too soggy to dig the pool.

Another thing you will find with Fair and Flexible clients is their willingness to give you leeway. They tolerate the inevitable bumps in the road; they don't hold it against you. They will show kindness and friendliness, and there is a human touch – for example, they understand that when it's hot outside, the workers might need a drink of water. They are the sort of people who will bring some out to them.

Fair and Flexible people will be accepting and under-standing about the inevitable hiccups that come as any project unfolds. They are reasonable and appreciate (and do not take for granted or expect) the extra-mile stuff you do. They won't come with a sense of entitlement, but with gratitude instead. Remember, these are the folks who will jump in and help dig the hole! They enjoy helping you – they will meet your team when they arrive in the morning, and I've even seen some of these customers help carry the supplies to the back of the house. They will make sure you have everything you need, and try to make your day pleasant. Their excite-ment about the project makes them a part of the team; they want to facilitate the entire process.

Another important factor for my business was Fair and Flexible clients made it possible for me to work more months out of the year. I had a very seasonal business, so it was great to find someone who'd let me schedule work during the fall or winter. I'd be looking to fill the calendar, and so I would offer a reduction in price if they could wait until after the height of the season or to build before the busy time started. Fair and Flexible customers would agree, even if it meant it would be months before they'd be able to use their pool. Those are the customers who kept my team working all year round.

I found that in the spring, even laid-back clients could get over-anxious, particularly if it got rainy and the project was delayed. During a week of rain, all the work I'd been in the middle of was on hold and new jobs had to be postponed. My Monday morning would be filled with calls from clients wanting to know when I'd be back (or starting) on the job. The customer who was understanding under these circumstances was worth more than any concession I might have made on price.

Let me point out that since I am so big on rapport, I felt that when people did get irritated at the wait, it gave me another chance to build our relationship. However, by building a pool in the fall, which the Fair and Flexibles allowed, everyone, the client included, would have a more relaxed experience. The customer wasn't straining at the bit to get out there and use the pool. For me and my team, the pressure of a deadline was lifted.

Fair and Flexible on the Job

Fair and Flexible clients were sensitive to my needs and those of my employees. They knew they were dealing with human beings, and not just a faceless business. These clients probably treated my employees the best (though Elite customers tended to be the best tippers!). Fair and Flexible people would be understanding about what we were up against. They might say things to me before I had to say it to them, for example, I'd get a call, "Hey Mitch we're having a lot of rain, we understand we're going to get delayed." That sort of flexibility goes a long way.

There are ways you can be flexible yourself during negotiations with a Fair and Flexible client like this, especially if you are pretty sure you want to work with them. For example, if they asked me to do better on the price, I would agree if they could wait a short time until a slower season. Think of some consideration that has importance to you, whether it is filling a slow schedule, like it was for me, or finding something that will help make your workday easier. Another way I might suggest they save money would be to hold off doing certain things, such as landscaping, instead of tackling the entire project (and expense) at once. It used to be that I could suggest people add their pool heater later to save some money, but now most people don't want to wait for warmer water! The key is turning the question into a chance to build rapport and trust. If you show your willingness to give and take, it will set the tone and establish both of you as fair and flexible.

Chapter Takeaway

A Fair and Flexible client:

1. Makes rapport-building easy as they also want to build a connection of trust.
2. Is helpful to you even though they hired YOU to serve THEM.
3. Is respectful of your workers, your effort, and your time.

7

THE RED FLAG

Y ou will regret this client. I feel so strongly that you should avoid this person that I am going to *start* with a list of red flags to watch for so you can recognize them:

1. They bully, badmouth, disrespect, or otherwise treat people badly.
2. They want to "cut to the chase" (meaning talk money) and have no interest in rapport-building.
3. They're rude to you or people who work for you. (No, it's not just a bad day.)
4. They have unrealistic expectations regarding price, schedule, and deliverables.
5. You can never fully satisfy them.

I used to say a **Red Flag** customer would "blame me for the rain." Out of all my customers I can say that in my experience, only a small percentage would stand out as the Red Flag, the worst kind of customer you can have.

Learning how to recognize them when you're sitting across from this stinker is one of the best things you can do for your company. They may start off looking like a Fair and Flexible, agreeable and friendly, but they change their stripes once the deal is signed and you are not getting an inch of latitude out of them after that. Sometimes they come across as a discerning Elite customer, demanding, exacting, but if they are unwilling to pay what it costs for me to provide the best possible outcome, they are not Elite. You will see their true colors when it comes to talking price. In the end, the worst-case scenario, you're going to cut your losses, telling them, "Don't pay me the last $5,000 you've been holding out, and never call me again!" You'll be glad to take money off the bill at the end and be rid of them.

Saying NO

Think of signing a deal as being on the peak of a hill. You've sweated, worked hard, made the climb, gotten the sale, and now you are shaking hands with a #3, the dreaded Red Flag. If you ignored your instincts and agreed to work with a Red Flag, it might look like you're on the top of the mountain, but in reality you are just a step from rolling downhill. You may have the sale but what else did you get with it? You probably shaved money off the bid in response to their hard haggling, but you figured you'd still do OK – you'd still make a profit. But, you're wrong. With this type of customer, you will wind up losing money on the contract. If they're a Red Flag, I'd rather send them to my competition.

I Smelled a Rat

My friend Tom, a longtime contractor, told me about how in the middle of a planning conversation, a customer got up and left the house without any explanation. I can imagine Tom sitting there with his mouth open in disbelief. He went ahead with the job and the problems added up. He was accused of making marks on the ceiling he hadn't made, and they blamed him for the spackle job, even though he hadn't *done* the spackling! He wound up losing thousands of dollars. In fact, the customers threatened to sue him if he pursued collecting the balance. Tom knew better, but he didn't listen to his gut and accepted the job anyway. In the end he blamed the customer for their rudeness, superior attitude, and for asking Tom to do inferior work. But Tom has some responsibility for the loss he took on this job.

I can't emphasize enough how listening to your gut will save you time and money. Saying yes in spite of your misgivings is never wise. How many jobs do you get out of ten prospects? If you tell me "ten," you're too cheap and likely not working with the right clients to build a happy business on. I think Tom learned his lesson over time. He told me that his uncle said many times,

"The jobs I made the most money on are the jobs I didn't get."

Trust

One of the signs you've met a Red Flag is they don't trust you. They make it clear in a number of ways. They challenge what you say as if you are trying to deceive them. They counter what you tell them by quoting things they read on the internet or heard from friends and other contractors. Another sign of lack of trust is not at all subtle: the prospect will talk about trust. For example, my dentist told me about someone who came in for a check-up and in their first conversation repeatedly asked, "Can I trust you?" and "How do I know that I can trust you?" He opted not to work with her, realizing that trust isn't measurable and someone who was this hesitant probably wouldn't trust him no matter what he said. A prospect may also tell you stories about why people in your industry are not trustworthy, based on experiences they have already had. Many seem skeptical of everything and everyone. It might be that trust is at the root of all the issues related to a Red Flag, I don't know. I'd say, don't try to convince them that you're the exception and that unlike everyone else you won't let them down. If they are expecting you to fail them, you may never be able to change that belief. Just walk away.

Expectations

Red Flag customers aren't happy with anything and their expectations are unreasonable. Of course, every homeowner has legitimate concerns and they expect a high-quality service when you are working around their house, but the Red Flags take it beyond that.

I have built pools for Red Flags who expected their pool to be more perfect than humanly possible. When you don't meet that impossible standard, they won't make their final payment. I saw my fair share of this #3 customer, mostly in my earlier years when I was still learning the ropes. I had one Red Flag who complained and disputed his final payment because his pool was one-quarter inch off level. Consider that we are talking about building swimming pools that were between thirty to fifty feet long, filled with thousands of gallons of water, installed against all the variations of soil and steel. The industry standard is two inches or less off level. That's "acceptable." Most companies try to build within one inch and we took great effort to do even better. It was unreasonable to expect more; the quarter inch was only visible with a ruler and a magnifying glass. The impossible requests are typical of the Red Flag clients. You can see there is no way to win with them. It isn't worth the aggravation or the money.

Who is the Expert Here?

My contractor friend Tom told me that he recognizes a Red Flag because they are confrontational and negative, right from the start. A Red Flag thinks they know more than you do. They tend to look for ways to prove you are wrong. They might use a random comment from someone whose situation is entirely different from their own to prove you should have done something differently. They find information online, use it to place blame on you, and to justify withholding money.

Sometimes it seems a Red Flag sets you up to fail. They believe they know your business better than you do, they watch your every move, and are suspicious that you are cutting corners, putting them last on the calendar, making excuses, and making mistakes.

All About the Money

Anyone who is shopping strictly on price is a #3. It's the most straightforward way to decide if they are a Red Flag. Don't fall for it if they tell you they've done a ton of research and spoken to six other companies so they already know all the other details. If they are only talking about the money, they are a Red Flag, not a Fair and Flexible who is doing their due diligence on cost.

I didn't sell on price. Whether I was the most expensive or not, I was proud to offer the best product on the market. I would even sell with that fact, focusing on excellence; how the client was getting the very best, paying for the top of the line. Don't get me wrong, I am not saying the most expensive contractors are necessarily the best – far from it! But I wanted to stand out and I charged what I needed to in order to serve people at that high level. I did things that other contractors didn't do in order to lengthen the life of a pool. I went the extra mile to ensure quality and longevity. For example, I would use thirty braces versus the eight most of my competition used. My competitors would sell against us, saying it wasn't necessary. They'd tell clients, "That's overkill! You don't have to pay for all that! You don't have to spend that much money." At the same time their contracts would read they weren't responsible if the pool emptied and it collapsed. Unlike any other vinyl pool out there, you could empty my pool and it would not collapse.

Fox Pools in York, PA, was the main supplier I worked with. It was a very unique company in the same way I wanted to be a unique contractor. I modelled my business on them. We stood for excellence and proudly charged what it cost to provide it. I had to pay more for a Fox pool, but they were simply the best. They were really a big part of my success and what made my company stand out from the rest. I worked with them for thirty-five years and in the process, they taught me a lot. They reminded me that price was not the most important thing and when I had a prospect so focused on what it would cost him or her, I learned rather quickly to let that prospect go. They'd be happier buying a lower quality pool at a cheaper price. Whoever was willing to sell a lesser product could deal with the endless complaints and problems that came with it.

The Unexpected

You could have the worst experience with a Red Flag, get finished, and be glad to never hear from them again. Then the strangest thing happens: they refer you. The client who calls based on that referral is potentially a great find. That's because they know how difficult their friend is to work with. They know he or she has unreasonable expectations. They know you must be at the top of your game to please that person. Of course, screen carefully, since they might be the same sort of obnoxious person, just looking for someone they can haggle with, harass, and hold out on. But I have rarely found that to be the case. If all goes well, before you know it, you're making money (indirectly) on a Red Flag. Plus, you might wind up with an added bonus, the reputation that you can handle the worst that someone can throw at you. Remember that possibility in the middle of your project with a Red Flag.

Interestingly, although a Red Flag might refer you to someone, for the most part my Red Flags didn't get my name from their friends I built a pool for. That's because my customers liked me. Either they didn't have Red Flags as friends or they weren't going to refer me to people who would put me in a difficult situation. They *liked* Mitch!

My old friend Steve told me that before he meets with someone who says they've been referred by a former client, he checks it out with them. He asks about the people before he schedules a meeting. Steve also Googles prospects and if he finds something concerning, he moves on because he's had his share of people that he wishes he'd never met. Steve says he has also left feed-back about people who turned out to be Red Flags, so that other contractors will know what they are getting into!

Uh-Oh, I Said "Yes"

On rare occasions you will finish a job for a Red Flag client and get out of there intact. Maybe you even made a small profit but you're most likely feeling, "I've had it with this guy! I want to rip his pool out!" There were occasions when we'd be done with a pool but the customer would be holding out payment, nitpicking about things we had no control over or responsibility for. I would take half the balance, knowing I'd never see him again.

John and Jane Doe (real names withheld for obvious reasons,) bargained me to the lowest price, but they said the things I wanted to hear and so I signed them. It turned out they were nothing like they seemed. They acted against my advice at every turn, and when it didn't work out well, as I warned them, they hated it and blamed me. In the end, they didn't pay in full.

If you're in bed with this client already, there's a few things you can do. If you are in conflict, stay calm. Calmness breeds calmness. Stay ahead of them when they call by having a couple of pieces of "good news" to share with them about how great the job is going and how beautiful it is going to be. This is one of the most successful ways to calm a Red Flag down. They're probably calling to tell you something negative, so disarm them with something positive. Keep in communication, even if you dread it. That means, take their calls and be honest as you keep them apprised of the project. Don't let too much time go by without touching base, because that list of things that are wrong will grow with every day you don't speak to him or her.

Can you turn a Red Flag around? In my opinion our personalities are set by the time we're six years old, so no. Neither can a client *become* a Red Flag after a bad experience with a contractor. A client once told a contractor friend, Richard, that she had "been ripped off to the tune of $100,000," by another construction company. Though Richard proved himself to be honorable and highly skilled, she turned out to be a nightmare to work with. She might have gotten ripped off once, but that wasn't what made her a Red Flag.

However, if someone tells you they've had a bad experience, that's not enough reason to label them a Red Flag. If you feel you have rapport with the client, they are accepting of the job and the price, and all they are showing is they feel a little hesitant, go ahead and tell them what you promise to do for them. Then, show them you are not that guy who hurt them in the past. As one happy customer said, "I was very leery but Mitch convinced me he is not one of those…"

When My Best Tactic Backfires

I mentioned how great it is when someone agrees to start their project in the fall when I have more time in my schedule. But Red Flag customers were especially rough about a fall install, even though I gave them a great price. To be fair, plenty of people have mixed feelings when they're being asked for a final payment on a $50,000 pool that they can't use for another six months. Their pool is done but their yard is a mess, the landscaping isn't in, there's no grass, and nobody can use the pool until next May. A lot of things would start to look like problems, including things that would be non-issues if it were June or July. I used to focus on the positive. "My guys told me this is one of the most beautiful pools we ever built!" Or, "Just think how great it's going to be when you open it. Wait and see how much fun you have with your family!"

I had to put my clients back in the mood they were in when they bought the pool – a time when they'd been to ten pool parties in a season and wanted that enjoyment for their own family. I might call and say, "I was by your house the other day, wait until the patio is in, this is going to be one of the best projects I've done all year!" I'd get them to visualize their kids jumping in the water, the party they would have for graduation, the relaxation of the pool at the end of a hot day.

If I was responding to complaints that seemed to be magnified because it was October, I would have to remind my customers, whether they were the genial Fair and Flexibles or Red Flags, why we made certain decisions. "Remember, we put the filter there for an important reason." The difference was the Red Flags could not be satisfied no matter how much I tried to put them back in the emotion of the buying decision.

Sometimes, if I was lucky, there might be the rare 90-degree October "Indian Summer" day forecast for that weekend and I'd be able to say, "Call me on Monday." After a weekend of using the pool, Fair and Flexible customers were appeased but the Red Flags were often not. To them it was simply a mistake to build when we did – and they blamed me for selling them on the fall install.

How to Recognize the #3

How do you tell you are about to enter a "Red Flag" relationship? Watch for the signs. Is the person smiling at you as they welcome you to the door, while kicking the dog out of the way? When the kids come over to the table during the appointment, are they snarling at them to leave us alone? How do they talk to their spouse? To the plumber who is just leaving?

If you can see they recently had work done – a new walk installed, a new kitchen, you can casually admire it and ask who did the work – and if your suspicions are strong, go ahead and call the contractor. Ask what this prospect was like to work for. Chances are many contractors within a fifty-mile radius knows about this customer.

You may not need to call – just listen to the prospect's answers. If you ask about the contractor who did the new walkway and they shower the company with praise, you might be OK. If they have nothing good to say and complain about the shoddy workmanship, the cost of the project, or how long the job took, beware. If you comment on how great the lawn looks and they tell you they've been through four landscaping services in eighteen months, watch out. It could be they were constantly firing companies – or it could be that the owners of those companies just got sick of taking abuse, late-payments, and other problems, and so they quit! If you ask the name of the person who did the work, and they don't want to tell you, that is a bad sign. It could be they treated them so badly they don't want to scare you off by giving you the chance to check.

If the prospect says things like, "the contractor missed a day," or "they wouldn't come in the evening," you might be dealing with someone who is unrealistic or overly-demanding. Are you willing to guarantee you'll never miss a day for any reason? Do you typically work in the evening or on the weekend? If that's your practice, you might be a great fit. Only you know what the warning signs of unrealistic expectations will be.

Another question you can ask is "How did you find out about me?" Print and Yellow Page ads were the most likely source for my #3s over the years. You can also preach who you are and see how they react. For example, I would tell them how I prioritize quality over speed and sometimes they would balk at that. If you hear they are worried about how fast you can be done, once the job is on, they will push you faster than you should go. In my business, if there were six days of rain it was not a good idea to do certain things in the back yard on the seventh day. When they insisted that I do things that went against my better judgement, I had to resist and not give in. I knew that the problems it would have caused would come back to bite me. That Red Flag customer would never acknowledge the role they played in pressuring you to go forward in spite of your best practices.

Ask and Tell

Here are some questions to consider when trying to identify a Red Flag.

- Do they care about what's best for both of you or are they only concerned with themselves?
- Do they negotiate or demand? For instance, "You have to build it next month!"
- Do they want a good job or a rush job? It's one or the other.

If you're still not sure, try the "Sell Your Quality First" approach. I'd tell my prospect,

"We need to let the ground settle a few days before we go on. We won't hurt the quality of your job, so we will wait for the right conditions." See how they reacted to that. If they said, "I get it but the pool has to be done in three weeks," that told me what I needed to know about working with them.

Tell them exactly how you run your business: "I always wait for my permits and inspections. I always wait for the right building conditions and use top quality, well paid employees." Someone who wants to rush and cut corners won't like to hear this. Pay attention to their reaction and trust your gut.

When it came to employees, I used to tell people, "You're going to love everyone who walks in your backyard!" I've been told that sentence meant more than anything to some clients. For others, skilled people who were respectful and considerate and took time to do things right were expected, but not worth paying for. You might find the Red Flag customer just doesn't care about the importance of quality workers. Once your people are on the job, they might not be treated the way you expect. You are going to have to be ready to speak up for them and insist on respect for your workers if necessary.

Trust your Gut

I wasn't sure that just saying "trust your gut feelings" was enough, but the more I talked to my colleagues for this book, the more often I heard it. For example, Jerry, who was my electrician for years, talked about prospects who were arrogant in pre-contract meetings and who gave him a hard time even before there was an agreement between them. He "knew" he should step away, but early on there were times he went against his better judgement, and later found out it was a mistake. As his career advanced, he learned to trust his gut, with better results. Jerry was careful to check out referrals. He'd call me or the referring contractor before meeting with prospects to be sure they were the kind of people he could work with.

There have been times I've walked into a home and been pretty hopeful. The place is beautiful, the signs are all there that they have money to spend, and I'd be optimistic. Then I'd sit down and all of a sudden, the client is yelling at their partner or ignoring the three-year-old who asks for a drink of juice. Learn the signs that point to a complicated, difficult customer and you'll know who to stay away from.

When you are new in business and just building a customer base, it is tempting to take everyone who is willing to hire you. I think it's far wiser – a better investment in your business, and your personal happiness – to figure out ways to turn down work. It's a learning experience. Look back at your past year. If you worked for a hundred people, think about the few you wish you'd declined. What did they cost you in terms of time, frustration, money, or loss of morale among your team?

Probably in the beginning you are going to have some Red Flags. Let them all be lessons learned. Over and over I saw it with friends who were running businesses – dealing with problems they could have avoided in the first place had they known which customers not to swing at.

I played some baseball in my younger days. When you are the hitter you have a sweet spot – the perfect place for a pitch to come in. All you have to do is swing. Sometimes it isn't getting the pitch right in the sweet spot that matters. It's knowing when not to swing at all.

Chapter Takeaway

Who should you have "passed" on this year? What would be different now?

8

REFERRALS

Most of us in business know referrals are a key to our success. If you're successful, you're probably doing some of this, even if not consciously. Being intentional about client cultivation means starting with the person right in front of you and people who you've worked with already.

When you attend to your clients, everything from your first impression to your first big issue (and you will have them, believe me) to your high-quality finished product matters. When you show how attentive you are to every phase of the project, your client will shower you with referrals, even though not every stage of the project goes perfectly. If you are engaged, aware of your client's feelings and needs, and you are connecting with them personally at every point, they will know you are on their side and trust that the issues will get resolved. In the end, they trust you to give them what they wanted when they signed on.

Customers will remember that you communicated,

responded to their problems, maintained rapport, and paid attention to what concerned them. Sometimes these are things they will tell their friends about – even more than they rave about the beautiful new pool, kitchen, or service you've provided. It is key to getting referrals.

Be Thinking of Who's Next

The very first thing you have to know about referrals is that you earn them. You first have to blow the socks off the people you're working for *right now*, because only when they're really happy will they recommend you to their friends, family, and co-workers. If you don't have a big roster of clients yet, and are working for a small and growing clientele, do everything you can to exceed their expectations. Meet their needs before they have to ask. Be better than the best: use your imagination to make them say, "Wow!" That is the very first thing you have to do in order to start a thriving referral business, which is hands down the best type you can have. Ideally you will build a business that grows based on referrals alone, without the need for advertising or even the use of social media (unless you get referrals from there too!)

One of my favorite clients was a very influential, successful, and wealthy guy who worked on Wall Street. By "wowing" him I gained access to many of the influential, successful, and wealthy Wall Street people he worked with every single day. When a potential client reaches out to you because a friend recommended you, that starts you off in a much better place than any other lead. You have a common friend. Think how much easier building rapport becomes when you have something to talk about: your mutual friend and how great it was to work with them. You also have credibility, social proof that you are trustworthy, effective, excellent. There's no better endorsement. When I can make a demanding client happy enough that they refer me to their friends, well that's a huge success to me.

Building the Base

How do you build up a strong roster of raving fans who are dying to give your name out to everyone who wants to build a pool? You start at the very first meeting with a new client. You are looking ahead, not to just getting this job, but to all the jobs this client will send your way in the future. You are looking at more than what you have to do to get this job, or complete it to their satisfaction. You must be asking, "What do I need to do to get this person to be so happy they refer me for a lifetime?" And, the answer will be different for every customer.

When you build rapport with the client, imagine the invisible crowd of clients behind them. They are lined up to shake your hand next. What do you have to do to clinch it?

There were times after the pool was installed that I had a chance to continue referral building. It happened quite a lot, actually. Let's talk about a new pool owner going through their first spring with their new pool. It has just rained for a week, the backyard is soaked, the water level is at the top of the pool, debris is in the pool from all the wind and rain. The homeowner was hoping to have their first pool party that past weekend but they had to cancel. The homeowner is upset, feeling a bit of buyers' remorse. What I have to do, if I want this customer to recommend me to a friend (and recommend building a pool!), is to get above the rain issue and remind them of what it felt like when they were dreaming of owning a beautiful pool.

First, I have to address their feelings. I understand their disappointment and I express my empathy. But then I have to turn it around. I ask them if they have rescheduled their party and I find out the date. I would tell them I will send someone by, at my expense, to get the pool cleaned up for their rescheduled party. This might cost me $100 in labor and chemicals, maybe less. I would call them the afternoon before the party to make sure everything is working. I would advise them to run the heater the day before to start to warm the pool and to make sure it was working as it should. I would offer to help them anyway they needed me to. Now, you have to realize this upcoming party is a way for you to not only build rapport with your homeowner but also an opportunity to meet people through your homeowner, many of whom are considering a pool down the line. I have the chance to build a great first impression with dozens of people I have not even met yet. By now the homeowner is bragging about me and my company, about my concern, and the extra things I did for them to help them prepare for the party. I am telling you less than one out of ten companies would do something like this, but there are few things that will build rapport with your homeowner faster than doing the unexpected. I've been thanked over and over for going beyond expectation and I've reaped the reward in referrals. The guests at the party see the beauty of the new pool, they hear about the extremely concerned builder, me, and that's a combination that is hard to beat. In what ways can you go over and above what is expected of you?

Deep Impact

Make a first impression that leaves an impact. My sales people were trained to always take their shoes off when entering someone's home. I did this too – I always made sure to wear nice socks! I wanted to show the customer that I was going to treat their home better than anybody else. What unique sort of thing can you do to show your respect for the prospect, your unique level of dedication, innovative style, or passion for your business right from the get-go? Let the image of my carefully chosen socks inspire you! Visualize me taking the unusual step of taking off my shoes as soon as I entered their home. How can you honor your prospects so that it makes an impression?

Once you've got the job, take every concern they bring you seriously. Value people's opinions and listen to their ideas, needs, and wants. Belittle nothing that concerns them, regardless of how illogical it may seem to you. I have seen how businesses do the stupidest things to ruin opportunities with customers. The biggest one is not taking the customer's feelings seriously. I always tried to, and it made a difference in my business. It proved my respect for my clients and that built their loyalty toward me. You may know the client's concern is not very rele-vant, but that doesn't matter. Don't waste time telling them it isn't important. If it doesn't cost you much to do what they're asking, just do it. Even if there is nothing you can do to "fix" a problem the client might see, you must show them you respect them and you are willing to listen. Show understanding instead of being dismissive and you will establish a relationship of mutual respect. A great recommendation is, "Mitch listened to me."

Start Here

If you want to begin building a referral-based business, you need to be working toward it from day one. Start now by focusing on every single detail on the job you're doing. We noticed how important the small things were. The client would appreciate it so much to see our tired guys sweeping the sidewalk at the end of every long, hot work day. They'd comment on it, it made them really happy and grateful. I'd also hear about it when someone on my team took time out to address a concern, for example, how the foreman quickly fixed something for them. Those types of things mattered almost as much as the beautiful sparkling pool we built in the backyard-and they set us apart from the competition.

We made sure to keep our customer's homes presentable knowing how messy a pool installation can be. It really made a difference in how smoothly the job seemed to go. Thoughtfulness builds referral customers. I say nothing is too small, but if you can make a bigger splash, that's even better. For example, there were times when I would finish a pool and it would be July 4th. Yes, we made the holiday deadline, but the backyard's a mess, there is dirt all around the pool, the grass hasn't grown back yet, and there's no patio. I used to bring in inexpensive indoor-outdoor carpeting, so I could turn this mess into something useable. It had an amazing effect on people.

Build on the Negative

You don't only get referrals because of the brilliant innovative ideas that make people smile. A complaint is a great opportunity to build a referral customer for life. Don't look at it as a pain in the neck – see it as a way to find creative solutions that will clinch a referral customer. Go back to rapport. Every problem has to be an opportunity. Another excellent opportunity is that moment of buyer's remorse I wrote about. You can empathize because many of us will experience it after a big purchase. Just when they can't find anything good about their purchase, you can help them remember their vision, their reason for building it, their dream. Turn around their thinking when they are really doubting and you have created a customer for life. If my clients were unhappy, I was unhappy. Starting from that point of view cemented my relationships in that moment and in the future. If my happiness is linked to theirs, they feel it. They know I have their best interest at heart. And, they know I am like that with everybody. Why wouldn't they refer me to their friends?

Always Available

We live in an always available culture with one-click access to almost anything. Now more than ever, calling people back quickly is important. Not doing so is damaging. I gave everyone my one and only cell phone number and told my clients they could call me any day, even on a Sunday, if they had a problem, if they couldn't get their heater on, for example. Many problems were solved over the phone with a little instruction. I would also have a couple of technicians on call as well, knowing that the worst thing is planning a party on a weekend and finding out there's a problem and you can't use the pool. I had one client who had a retractable cover on his pool and on the weekend of a big party, he couldn't open it. My guy got the pool cover open and that homeowner referred me so often after that, it was just that important to him.

Opportunities from Start to Finish

After the job is done you can continue creating a customer that will give you a lifetime of referrals. You've finished the job and won't be there every day anymore, but you still have this golden opportunity. When the job is done there's so many simple things you can do. Make a follow up call to see if everything was done to their satisfaction. You'd be surprised how few contractors think to do this. Maybe they are afraid they'll hear complaints and they'll find themselves back on a job they thought they'd finished. But if that happened, I would see it as another chance to make a great impression, to deepen the relationship and prove my quality to this client, and by extension to everyone they will refer me to later on down the line.

I suggest you call and ask, "Was there anything I could have done better?" You will get an education, and you will show your client how diligent you are. A lot of business people will never take this advice and make this call. We are so afraid to hear something negative about ourselves or our business, and we are afraid things might cost us time and money. But imagine the impact of a phone call a week after the pool's done, where you ask how the pool is. If they had questions or problems that you can easily answer or solve, you might prevent negative comments to their friends via the phone or on social media.

You can make it a practice to send someone out to make sure everything is functioning properly and to help clients with any of their questions. Don't let that checkup visit go unnoticed. Tell them you'll be dropping off a helpful guide to understanding the chemicals, and "What's a good time to stop by?" That's clinching the referral. It doesn't mean you're looking for a problem, but by addressing things quickly you can turn lemons into the lemonade. People remember you for it.

There were times when someone would tell me, "Well, I wasn't going to mention it, but since you called…" This nice person was going to live with that little bit of disappointment. That's corrosive. By calling I removed anything that could get in the way of a full-throated endorsement of my work. No disappointments mean no hesitation when someone asks for a referral. By calling, I gave a really nice person who didn't want to "bother me" the chance to feel completely satisfied with my level of customer care. And, that satisfaction is exactly what wins you referrals from a really nice person who probably has really nice friends.

I Heard From My Friend

When you walk into the home of a customer who was referred to you it is a whole different experience from your other leads – your selling is half done for you. You didn't have to advertise and your reputation precedes you. The way you build that sort of reputation that creates enough referral to sustain a thriving business is to only be happy when your customers are happy. Then, make it your priority to bring the happiness.

Be unlike most of the other contractors out there and care about the client beyond the job. Your referral building work is not done just because the job is over. When do you ask for a referral? Never ask. Just make working with you so good that the customers can't help but sing your praises to their friends. Make the experience that good. Let everything you do clinch the next referral. Because when a friend raves about you, it is worth more than all the pay-per-click ads you can buy.

Chapter Takeaway

A referral is built from the very first meeting with a prospect to the follow up at the end of a job with the prospect who's become a faithful customer. Even issues that arise are ways to create clients and referrals for life.

9

GETTING PERSONAL

Passing on the Headaches

Maybe you're thinking you won't be the one handling the complaints, it'll be the people on the job or at customer service. If that's your attitude, you might as well stop reading now. The businesses I want to serve love their employees and take everyone's satisfaction into consideration. I saw my employees as members of my family and the right clients became extended family who would make my business a pleasure and be ambassadors to their friends and neighbors. If you can make that mental shift and treat your business like a family you're building, the idea of being careful about who you work with will make more and more sense. Keeping your family happy becomes part of your business plan.

Maybe you're not the one bringing in the customers, your sales force is. Help the sales team learn the value of a good solid "no thanks," even with what *looks* like a profitable lead. Forgive, even praise them for passing up that sale, and understand why they did it. Not only will you forgive them, you'll thank them in the end, and I suggest you might give that sales person a little bonus for coming back to you and saying, "We don't want these people as our clients!"

A salesperson who does that is turning down a commission, which has a bigger impact on them than you. How great would it be for you to say, "So, here's a little bonus for saving us a lot of headaches."

Face to Face to Facebook

Building a reputation one client at a time is a basic principle of sales. In my mind, one at a time is also how you weed out the turkeys. Unfortunately, the kind of one-on-one, in-person interaction I did on a regular basis and which I recommend is harder and harder to do. Nowadays you don't even have to buy a car from a human being. You can select it from a website and pick it up from a car vending machine!

If you are a business owner in a service-oriented field, you still have the opportunity to meet your clients face to face, and I believe that is the best way to build a solid business. In this case, if you have a brick and mortar storefront or showroom, you might have an advantage. If you can get people in the door, you can meet and mutually decide whether you're a good match. If you don't have a store, there are other ways to get into the marketplace and interact with the public. For example, I attended home shows with as many members of my team as I could. We'd bring giveaways and be available for casual conversation as much as for Q and A about our pools. Along the same line, a friend of mine who is an editor volunteers at writer's conventions so she can interact with prospects for her services. As Farmer's Markets are springing up all over the place, I've noticed not everyone is selling vegetables. There are people offering everything from catering services to roofing at Farmer's Markets. For the price of renting a table, they are having hours of conversations in person with potential clients.

After an initial contact, whether it was at a home show or at our showroom, I would meet people at their homes whenever possible. Being in person did not just give me the chance to show them better who I am, but also gave me an opportunity to see if *they* fit *me*. In my business, just because someone wanted a new pool was not enough reason to work with them. I wanted to know it was going to be mutually beneficial, and not only financially. The reason I suggest you do the same is: it works.

Was meeting face-to-face foolproof? No, of course some difficult people snuck through because either I failed to "read" them or they were working hard to convince me they'd be agreeable, easy to work with and friendly, when in fact they were anything but.

If you can't sit down across the table with your prospect, at least have a phone conversation. You want to give the prospect a chance to see what it would be like to work with you, and you are looking for that same information. You want to build rapport so you can not only sell yourself, but also get to know who you're dealing with so you can make an informed decision about whether you want to work with them or not.

About Advertising

So much gets lost in these days of Facebook ads and sales funnels. Business owners hope that if they throw enough pay-per-click ads out there, people will call. It's today's version of print ads in flyers and circulars. Of course, there are definitely sales that come in through this "spray and pray" method. But I have found a significant number of clients I should have avoided over the years came from print ads. I found good customers from the print ads, don't get me wrong. But, far and away the most satisfying relationships came from face-to-face interactions – and, those that came to me via print advertising were quickly followed up by an in-person meeting.

Getting Reviewed

OK, so you're intrigued. Maybe you're thinking you do have some say in who you work with. You might even agree that building relationships first and choosing the right people (not just anyone who finds you) has some validity. But people are searching online for everything from pools to dentists. The first time your prospect "meets" you is probably not even on your own website but on a review site that pops up on a Google search. Quite possibly, it's a site that has information and reviews you have never even seen.

You understand how important reviews can be. It's hard to imagine not checking reviews before buying a dishwasher, reserving a hotel, or taking a trip. It would be like living without weather forecasts. If you wonder if you should go to the beach, you check your phone and if it says rain by noon, you go to a movie instead. Wondering if you should drive from New York to Boston today? Not if there is a snowstorm in the forecast. Not that meteorologists or review sites are always right, but we all tend to check in with them anyway.

Review sites can work for you. They are places where live conversations are happening. Be a part of the conversation. You want to know what is being said about you online because your reputation can go down the drain with just a few bad reviews. But you can make sure negative reviews don't stay out there on the web forever. Look at them as an opportunity to correct issues, restore rapport, and rebuild trust. Your goal should be that an unhappy customer is willing to revise their review and observers are impressed by your generosity and desire to work it out.

A good practice is to reply to all comments whether they are positive or negative. It builds trust with prospects when you acknowledge both. Only get involved in an online conversation if you can avoid getting hostile or defensive, which just makes matters worse and turns off anyone else who is shopping for your services online.

Review sites are a fact of life. Though it means you have less control over a potential client's first impression, it doesn't mean you are out in the cold. The goal is to maintain an active, professional, responsive presence online, and direct prospects to your website, where you have more control over what they see. Whenever possible, encourage people to reach out to speak to you or your representatives personally.

If you get a call from an internet lead and you feel the people are probably folks you would like to meet with, make an appointment to meet at their home, if possible. Even though they did not come to you as a referral, you may be able to make them one. I used to keep a list of 500 satisfied clients, organized by town. Early in my presentation we would look at the pages for their town and often there was someone they knew on the list – sometimes, even more than one. Once this would happen, they would turn into a referral after the fact, knowing that I had made their friends or neighbors happy.

When you follow up on an internet lead, begin rapport building immediately and prequalify the prospect. What are they like? Is it a true lead? Sometimes I would receive calls from people who were moving out of the area and were just looking for information. Other times they would say they are years away from actually building a pool (if at all,) and other times they would say they are looking for the best price. In all these cases I knew this was not a lead for me. I would graciously thank them for contacting us and wish them the best.

If you prefer reaching out to prospects virtually, fine. Let the customer warm up to you by reading good reviews and comparing you to your competition online. But have your salesperson ready. Because once that click through from your website happens, somebody has to follow up with a call or the in-person visit. Don't rely on an auto-responder email to do it for you. Either become the person who can build the personal relationships or send your best salespeople – the true "people person," who makes friends everywhere they go, lets rejection roll off like water, and who truly enjoys the face-to-face meet-ings that will be key to your (and their) success. You might even give them this book and also give them permission to use it – by turning down people they sense will be difficult to work with.

Referring Friends

There were times when I wound up working with some stinkers because they came in via referral from someone I liked. I had a belief that birds of a feather flock together, so most of the time I trusted the referral would be just as kind, warm, and easy to work with as their friend, and they just weren't. Overall however, I'd encourage you to trust your referrals. They are already leaning in your direction, based on their friend's experience. It's like they want to be your friend too.

In spite of the few stinkers who squeezed through, I still believe in-person interaction is best for building a client base you will love. I heard from a friend who recently attended a business-building group and the advice was the same. Don't settle for outreach at a distance: not ads, emails, or instant messages. Get on the phone and give the client an experience. Show them who you are and figure out who they will be if you choose to work with them. Then, trust that as those satisfied customers will tell their like-minded friends about you, your business will shift toward being referral-based. That was key for me; eventually close to ninety-five percent of my sales came from referrals which meant I could pick and choose, and I never had to "spray and pray" again.

10

FELIX UNGER ON THE JOB

You may not be old enough to remember The Odd Couple, a TV show about two divorced guys who live together in New York City. One is a slob, Oscar Madison, played by Jack Klugman, and the other is a neat-freak, Felix Unger, played by Tony Randall. Felix is the one who noticed every crumb or speck of dust and it drove him crazy. That's the nickname my team gave me: Felix. They knew that the moment I showed up on a job site, I'd start cleaning up. I set an example for my workers. I didn't just point to messy parts of the walkway and tell my staff to clean it, because I was not above them. I'd sweep the sidewalk as fast as anybody. I preached neatness to my employees and they'd tease me about it, but those things matter because clients notice. Soon my staff would see the mess without me seeing it first, that would reflect well on them, on me, on the project, and on the business. Felix is that old saying "Cleanliness is next to Godliness," times ten.

I think being aware of being neat and clean is especially important at the end of the day. People are coming home from work or starting their evening routine. They find that the place is clean. They see they're going to get their home back for the rest of the day, and they appreciate that.

If you've ever had work done in your home, you know how much turmoil it can cause. Your house is turned upside down – your whole life feels disrupted. But, if you've ever had a contractor clean up at the end of each day, sweeping up the dust from drywall, putting back the furniture they had to move, taking their tools away with them – it makes a big difference. You get your house back. The job might not be done, but you feel more comfortable. You're not tripping over extension cords. Most important: your contractor shows she or he cares about you and you're going to remember that.

You will find that your client can accept a certain amount of disruption – even more than they would otherwise – if you respect the fact that they still have to live there. They appreciate your extra effort. That was a top priority with me in my business, and when the inevitable hiccup came along during the job, I had built up that goodwill – which goes a long way.

If you go into people's homes or yards and know you're going to cause disruption just by what you are building or repairing, think about the additional stress you leave them with when you wrap up for the day and drop everything right where you moved, used, or worked on it. Now something comes up out of your control. Are they understanding or do they blame you? Never give a client the chance to say:

"They were disorganized and messy throughout the whole process. No wonder the project took two weeks longer than they said!"

People make correlations. If you are a slob on the work-site, they're going to assume you're probably disorganized with your billing, your subcontractors, your permits, and all the rest. Don't let them make that corre-lation about you.

Nowadays we are told to think about branding. Every-thing has to be consistent across your entire business. Make neatness, organization, and consideration of the client a part of your overall branding. Let it be part of your "message" and it will spread as your reputation. It's good for business.

Will your team call you "Felix?" Yes, it's an effort to take the tools out and to move the equipment to an out-of-the-way place, but teach them that they are building goodwill that will pay off – for them and for the company. Who knows, it may even pay off in the form of tips from the client, cold drinks on hot days, and forgiveness of the mistakes or delays that are part of any job.

Make sure to call people back quickly, and if necessary, get a service person on site quickly if something isn't working properly. So, whether or not you're a Felix Unger type, you can become a listening type. You can take people's worries seriously, even if you doubt anything bad will happen. You can tell them what you plan to do to solve the problem, even if you think it's an unnecessary fix. And you can be sure this sort of atten-tion to detail and respect for the customer's comfort and peace of mind will pay you back handsomely.

Chapter Takeaway

1. A neat job will seem like a better job than a messy job of the same quality
2. Don't underestimate the power of clean

11

THE $100 CLOSE

I mentioned that I have a technique that lets me close even the most iffy sales. It has worked for me for decades because it asks very little of the client, while allowing them to explore without fear or risk what it will be like to invest in a pool with me. It gives the people more time to think about things – and I have found by going this route, most often I'd speak to them a few days later and in their minds, they had already bought their new pool. I call it the $100 Close.

Overall, I had a very soft sell, which people appreciated. The $100 Close strategy was part of that. It didn't require a large deposit or commitment. The prospect wouldn't be obligating themselves to a contract, but all of the pieces would be falling into place as if they were.

Here is how the $100 Close works. Before you leave from your appointment, you simply offer to "write it up." You put a hurdle behind them. Writing up and signing a big long contract is a drag. I kept my contracts very simple so they were easy to complete. I'd say, "If we spend five minutes doing it now, and you decide you want to go ahead, then this part is already done."

I would write up the simple agreement and ask for $100. I would not call it a deposit, however, because that word carries a lot of weight and they might not be that far along in their thinking yet. They are starting to have an experience of working with me and I want it to be pain- and stress-free. I wanted them to enjoy it.

I might say, "You will have the contract in your hand so you can look it over. You can give me $100 to hold everything, and it is fully refundable."

Memorial Day and July 4th are the two holy holidays in the pool business. Clients want to be using their pools by one of these two dates. I had a policy that no matter how close we were to either of the holy days, I would not press them to make a decision. I wouldn't warn them that they were going to miss the upcoming summer, or that other buyers were going to squeeze them out of the schedule. I would not threaten in-season price increases. Instead, I offered them the softest of the soft sells. I would say,

"If you want, I can hold your place in the schedule, so you can have the pool installed this year, but you can keep thinking about it. See if it's right for you. If that sounds good, we can write it up and you can just give me $100, completely refundable to hold your place. If at any time you decide not to go forward, I will refund your money with no questions asked, no problem."

They would look at each other, and say, "Well, we're not committing to anything…"

But, psychologically, they were. I would slide that single

page agreement into a binder filled with pictures of beautiful pools and excellent referrals about me and my business. They could take some time finalizing their thoughts. They had a fully refundable $100 investment and that was it. It was such a comfortable way to end the meeting. If they changed their mind, there was no contract to tear up. It let them feel like what it would be like to buy from me without making a commitment.

The magic happened after I left the house with that check for $100. I was giving them time to think — but that $100 was a link to me and it functioned like a commitment. Often within a few days they'd call me up and ask when we were starting. They'd sold themselves.

It seems paying that nominal amount of money signaled their brain that a sale had taken place — and there was a pool on the way. From then on, they acted like there was a plan: a contract, an agreement. They'd get super-excited for their pool, and we'd be on our way.

I used this strategy for decades to turn fear into anticipa-tion — because once you can get the customer past dreading the sales transaction, into thinking about the rewards to come, imagining their family enjoying their beautiful new pool together, the sale was clinched. You didn't have any buyers' remorse because they haven't spent the money, but they got to dream as if they had. They can imagine the pool as a reality and now, there is only one small step to actually owning the pool they've been dreaming of.

The $100 is just enough to make them feel like money has changed hands — but not so much as to be scary, unlike a twenty percent deposit. And I would not use the word "deposit." I'd say, "The $100 holds your place in the schedule," or it "holds the price I quoted you today."

If you try this technique, remember, it has to be a low (nominal) amount, but something that is still meaningful – it will be the connection to you and not the other guy. Lots of people walk away from offers to "think about it," and if they aren't tied to your particular offer in any way, there's no reason *not to* continue the search with someone else. This, on top of the amazing first impression you made, and the quality of your product or service, will close the deal.

I mentioned that it's a way to feel how it'll be to work with you – so here's your chance to show them. It might take more than a day, so take that time to prove how good it can be to work with you. Be available to them, follow up, leave giveaways to remind them of the great meeting you had and the opportunity they have to enjoy the benefits of your product.

The $100 Close was the first step. My prospect wasn't rushing into a sale, they were exploring the possibility. This technique let the homeowner come along with me psychologically. They could try on the idea of a pool as well as the idea of working with me. Once a prospect gave me that $100, I was ninety-five percent of the way to installing their pool.

Put it in Writing

The other thing that moved my sales along were the very simple one-page proposal that I wrote up and left for my clients. It drove me nuts when other pool companies created these long, confusing proposals that added things that didn't matter. I didn't do that. I had really easy-to-understand proposals, one-sheet that just said, "you're getting this size pool, this is the price, and these are the accessories" – very easy. That meant a lot. It helped people get past the pricing. And I never saw a proposal that was even close to mine. We were the best vinyl pool company, everything we did we chose for the best outcome. If the pipe I used was the best, most long-lasting pipe, and it was the most expensive, nobody appreciated or understood that. Other companies would write that in, "We use 200 of the best copper nails on earth." Those who put all those mind-numbing details into their proposals were not giving the best, they were covering for what they weren't doing! If you have to "pad" it, what are you holding back?

YOUR $100 Solution

The $100 Close gave my prospect the chance to see who they are dealing with, to feel the experience of buying a pool, and what they are agreeing to before committing to the sale. It became the *only* way I would close a sale. And if I didn't want to work with someone, I would not bring out this option at all. It was only for someone I wanted to work with. Of course, there are alternatives to this low-pressure technique, so find one that works for you best. For a coach it can be several free no-pressure sessions, where you give your best and they feel your commitment to serving them. Whatever it is, the goal is to give the client an experience of working with you at your best: flexible, easy-going, professional, and friendly.

Sales Tools You Can Touch

I mentioned that I used to come to each prospects' home with a three-inch binder to leave with them. At the start of the season I'd have an inventory of binders printed up. They were impressive, nice to look at, and chock-full of powerful, persuasive information. One of the key ingredients was that printed recommendation list, organized by town, with 500 names on the list, and that social proof and credibility was very persuasive. On the list fifty of the clients were happy. Four hundred and fifty of them were raving-lunatic happy. Part of the pitch was going through this list together. That recommendation list sold pools for me. I'd show them the prospects on the list, which was organized by town, and there was always someone they knew close by.

"Oh! You did the Smith's pool? I know them!" And, after I left the house, they would make a call to the Smiths to talk about their experience with me. Sometimes just seeing their acquaintance's name there on the list was enough. Probably most of the time, it was enough. Seeing a friend or two on my list would turn the prospect into a referral. I might even suggest we call their friend or acquaintance right then and there. "Let's give them a call and see what they say about me!"

Today you'd do it all online maybe, but I think there is something to be said for handing out the giveaway with the hard proof right in front of the potential customer while you are sitting there. About the binder I will say, don't show this sort of thing until you feel like you've got rapport. The list is an extension of the rapport; you are talking about the people you worked for and the relationship you had with them. It is personal, and you don't want to do that until your prospect trusts and likes you.

To back up the power of the list, I had a hundred letters of recommendation, thanks, and praise that my prospects could read through. Please use all the letters you receive. Don't just hang them on your wall, or God forbid, throw them away.

I showed my prospects my five hundred recommendations, my one hundred letters of rave reviews and pictures of all the beautiful pools they could have in their yard before the swimming season began. We'd enjoy each other's company, deepen our rapport, maybe make a call to someone on the list to establish my credibility. Then, I'd leave the binder on the table.

"You're leaving this binder with us?" they'd ask.

I knew they would pore over everything in there – the pictures, the letters, and the names. I sold a lot of pools with that binder.

Get Creative

Especially for first-time pool buyers, I had to show them what it would be like to enjoy the benefits of owning a pool as well as the benefits of choosing me to be the one to build it. I was very aware that while I was building rapport, the homeowner was observing me, and more importantly, they were trying to visualize working with me. It was my job to help them see it. Visualization was especially important for the amateur who never bought a pool before and they are looking at a very big expense. How could I help them see it?

Pools come in several typical shapes. One of the ways I helped them to see what a pool would look like was I had tarps pre-cut in the sizes and shapes of my pools which I would lay out where the pool might go. I'd bring my prospects out into the yard to see where they could put their new pool. We'd have fun with it, move lawn furniture all around it, letting them see what it would be like when the pool was installed. I would leave the tarp with them for a few days. Soon they'd be calling to tell me how they were out there later that day moving the pool around some more. They were getting excited about their new pool, which was becoming more of reality with the image the tarps created. Plus, they'd had the experience of me out there with them, having fun, moving their patio furniture around to see where the pool would look best. I was part of their positive experience already, and since I was sincerely having fun too, just being myself, my prospective clients could feel our rapport was natural and authentic.

Chapter Takeaway

My $100 Close was the bridge for my clients from thinking about it to owning it. What is the equivalent of your $100 Close?

12

TAKING CHARGE OF THE
EXPERIENCE

Nobody likes to be sold to, but a lot of us appreciate a little guidance as we begin an unfamiliar process. What if you started to look at sales as guiding clients in a process toward the right buying decision?

Here is how I guided my prospects through the process of buying a pool. I'd begin by taking my time to build rapport, sometimes over several visits. I wanted to be seen as a friend with something to offer, not a stranger or a salesman. Taking my time helped them imagine working with me.

All this time building rapport wasn't manipulation or solely for the client's benefit either. You are deciding whether this is a prospect you want to work with. Taking this time is to your advantage.

With the $100 Close, I was guiding my customers to experiment with and experience being a pool owner without all the finality and commitment. I further

MITCH CANTOR

guided their experience by helping my prospects see the outline of a pool in their yard, using tarps and turning it into a game we all played together. I was a big fan of this kind of sales aid. We'd place the "pool" wherever we liked it, and put their very own patio furniture all around it. Or, what the heck, they might decide, this stuff isn't good enough! We'll get all *new* patio furniture! Stuff that would be worthy of the gorgeous new pool they were about to install.

Why do car dealerships want you to take a test drive? Because they hope that after you've driven the car, sat in those comfortable seats, had a chance to see how beautiful the car is, and how great it drives, you will be more likely to buy it.

I was in the home improvement business. There was a lot for a homeowner to consider when it came to buying a pool, so much so that it was hard to make final decisions quickly. Colors, size, shape, location, and a host of other questions relative to the project had to be answered. For these reasons it was hard to ask for an order on the first meeting. But I didn't want to leave without doing something to get the client started on thinking about hiring me. Much of what I did was giving them a "test drive."

I also liked to guide the in-person meetings. I was often seeing a husband and wife. More often than not, one wanted to build the pool and the other didn't. The majority of the time the wife wanted it and the husband was only thinking about the money. I understood it this way: Mrs. wanted it because she realized the joys of having the pool, the parties, videos of their friends coming over, keeping the kids active all summer. She

100

knew what a pool would add to the dimension of the home, in terms of value and enjoyment. Mr. was only thinking, "It's going to be $50,000 to do this to my backyard."

I would use this awareness in my pitch, concentrating on helping the person who wanted it the least to imagine the benefits. Often, once it was built, the person who was the most resistant was the one to call and tell me, "I wanted it the least, but I think I enjoy it the most!"

The Kitchen Table Experience

When I met with people in their homes I wanted to sit at the kitchen or dining room table. I wanted to be at the head of the table, in the middle so I could talk with everyone equally – I didn't want to be on the opposite side of the table, it felt very adversarial: them against me. I wanted to remove that dynamic of opposition. Sitting in between a couple literally and symbolically put me in a different position in relation to them, and it changed the flavor of the conversation. It created a team, and made us all feel connected.

There was always a moment when I knew we crossed the rapport line. The conversation became very relaxed. People opened up and started to tell me stories of their life. They might say something like, "We could talk all night, but it must be time to show us your pools." It wouldn't feel like I was there to sell a pool but to start a new friendship. This moment was very satisfying for me. The sale had begun.

Sometimes the dynamic shifted when one of the family members would offer me a coffee or a glass of iced tea.

They were leaving their partner alone with me at the table, vulnerable to my persuasion! I never took advantage of that, but it always gave me a sigh of relief. My prospect felt I was "safe" to leave with their partner. Nothing terrible or irreversible was going to happen if we were left alone. Sometimes I took it as symbolically giving me permission to work with their more reluctant partner. I knew we'd gone a couple of steps closer to the sale.

13

GO THE EXTRA MILE AND CHARGE
WHAT YOU'RE WORTH

I n the introduction I promised to tell you about a "how" that is really just a simple commitment that will benefit you for years to come if you decide to make it. That commitment is to being completely true to yourself and your own brand of excellence. You are different from every other business out there. Go ahead and charge what it costs to provide your unique brand of excellence. If you decide to be at the high end of your industry you have nothing to apologize for. Believe in your product or service, determine to be the best, and charge what it costs to do business at that level. It is a simple, important statement about your values that you don't settle, cut corners, or hold "close-out" sales. Charging a premium isn't only for the premier Elite client. Being the best, even if that means you become one of the most expensive out there is O.K. People will appreciate you for it. Not everyone, but you don't want to work with "everyone."

When you can talk about who you are and what you do

without any sort of attitude – apology *or* bragging – you will be giving the best of yourself and your business, it will become about service at the highest level, and people will appreciate it. Don't allow marketers (sales gurus) to tell you how to appeal to everyone. You don't want to work that hard. Find your niche, your Elite and Fair and Flexible clients, and focus on making their experiences with you amazing. Then, fire the sales gurus and run your referral-based business for the sheer joy of working with people you love.

I got to the point where I sold a pool in part because I didn't want the customers to have to deal with the competition. That's how much better I knew I was. That's how much I came to love the people I worked with. I knew they'd have a great experience with me and I was determined they would have it. Nobody else could do it better so I was obligated to sign them up or else I was throwing them to the wolves!

Going the extra mile goes hand-in-hand with the idea of knowing your value and being willing to ask for what you're worth. It means staying attentive throughout the entire project and then calling after the project is done to ask how things are. Ask if there are any concerns you can address and do it. Send them some additional, helpful information about the product you sold them, something beyond what comes with the "kit." Show genuine interest. Love them to death. By doing these things you are clinching the next referral and standing heads and shoulders above the rest. Is the market full of the type of service you provide? Maybe. Is it full of people willing to work for the "wow?" Absolutely not.

CONCLUSION

What's the Take-Away?

So, did I help your business? Even better, did I make going to work a pleasure? Maybe not yet, but if you see now that *who* you choose to work with is as important as *how* you run your business, you may realize that there is a way to make your life much easier.

Whether you're starting, growing, or keeping the flow of your business going, apply what you read in this book and you will see your business profit and satisfaction go way up. You can even make going to work a pleasure. Just choose the right people to surround yourself with and you will see the difference. Red Flags will fade away because you can spot them a mile off. The crazy-happy customers will be the ones singing your praises and have you raking in their referrals. You'll get better and better at building rapport, and you'll let go of any hesitation you may have about eliminating the impossible customers. Who knows, without all the stress they brought, you might wind up being more creative and innovative in your business, as I found I was.

Now, I know we're not supposed to blame others, and of course when you're in business, the buck stops with you. Leaders who realize that take full responsibility. That's admirable. But I hope you've seen that you can take some of the pressure off yourself when you realize the success or failure and the pleasure or pain of your business is *not* all you. Sometimes, it actually *is* the customers you choose to work with.

A client who demands too much without rightfully paying you for the extra time, attention, labor, and materials is a drain on you, your team, and your business. And, there really is no way to tally the cost of aggravation, tension, stress, and time spent in defending, arguing, appeasing, or placating a hard-to-satisfy client. Why take them on? Keep in mind you are the one who picks "the other guy," just the way you pick your employees. Make sure they are the right individuals for YOU.

In the beginning you may have to take some jobs you're later going to be able to turn down. But don't build your business on those. See them as springboards to the day you can "pass." See them as a way to learn:

- What signs do I see that tell me this client will drain my energy, time, and money?
- What do I notice about how they communicate with me and with each other, when I am in their home?
- What do they say about other contractors they've worked with?

- What's their reputation? Who referred them and what did they tell you about them?

And the bad choices? The jobs you wish you'd turned down? See those jobs as feedback. Let them teach you what happens when you work with customers who are impossible to please, the ones with the track record with every other service provider or contractor all over town.

What's the take-away for you, the business owner? Be a people-person. Not in the sense of forcing yourself to be outgoing or become something you're not. But keep a keen eye on the people you bring into your life as employees, salespeople, and clients. Become a people person in that you can "read" people: what they will be like to work with, and how you can best serve them.

You may have to teach your sales team some of what you've learned. Teach them to trust their gut. Praise and reward them for watching out for the entire company by avoiding Red Flags.

Customer-Friends

I always looked at my business as a family – that includes my customer-friends. I was always trying to build a family atmosphere and everything I did was to foster that. How I treated people, both team members and customers, made all the difference. Even though I am retired, I still maintain a lot of relationships with people who were my customer-friends. Thanks for becoming one of those by reading this book. I wish you success in your business and your life!

ABOUT THE AUTHOR

Mitch Cantor

Mitch Cantor, author of *It's the Other Guy: Say Goodbye to Bad Clients and Hello to Bigger Profits and a Better Life* is the founder and past President of Sun Design Pools, which reached Inc. 5000 status as "one of the fastest growing small companies in America." Mitch is an award-winning industry leader in home improvement with forty years of experience running his multimillion-dollar company in New York.

From young entrepreneur to enthusiastic business owner, Mitch says his company "gave him everything he was looking for." He offers you a chance to say the same about your own business. If you are in service to others, this book will help you to succeed and to love the process.

As an author, Mitch carves out new territory, teaching his readers how working with the right people will allow you to enjoy success and avoid frustration. He says, "I learned to stay away from those who would make my life hell, and I have shared these secrets with you in this book."

Mitch is also a songwriter and independent music producer, having the pleasure to work with so many talented artists as you can see on mitchcantor.com.

Today Mitch and his wife Marla divide their time between Boca Raton, Florida and Jericho, Long Island. Retirement is the fruit of their labor, and as Mitch puts it, "retirement is treating us well "

Together Mitch and Marla enjoy traveling and seeing nature's beauty, watching young and seasoned music artists perform, and continuing their own music and book writing. Mitch's family always was and remains his top priority, the inspiration of it all.

Thank you for Reading!

If you could please take a moment to leave a quick review of the book (http://tiny.cc/ItsTheOtherGuy), that would be extremely appreciated!

I look forward to connecting with you.

facebook.com/mitch.cantor.3

twitter.com/MitchCantor

instagram.com/mitchcantor1

Made in the USA
Middletown, DE
19 February 2020